Learn
Universal Horse Language
No Ropes

by Hertha James

Powerword Publications,
Palmerston North, New Zealand
Muddy Horse Coaching
hertha.james@xtra.co.nz
www.safehorse.info
www.herthamuddyhorse.com

© Hertha L. James (2016)

Font: Bookman Old Style 11

Disclaimer of liability:

The author and publisher shall have neither liability nor responsibility to any person or entity with respect to any loss or damage caused or alleged to be caused directly or indirectly by the information contained in this book. While the book is as accurate as the author can make it, there may be errors or omissions.

Horses that show dangerous behaviors should not be paired with casual or inexperienced horse owners or handlers. Readers are entirely in charge of their own actions.

Risk Radar: When around horses, we must have our Risk Radar on at all times.

Cover Photo by Hertha James, features Smoky greeting his person.

Photography by Bryan James, Hertha James, Bridget Evans unless otherwise stated.

Some of the photos are taken from video footage, which decreases quality but allows illustration of an exact moment or exact movement.

Learning is a thing that follows us around
for the rest of our lives.
Chinese Proverb

Other Books

Other Books by this author are available, as e-books or as hard copy books, from Amazon.com.

They contain extensive background material and specific Training Plans.

- ➢ *How to Begin Equine Clicker Training: Improve Horse-Human Communication*

- ➢ *Conversations with Horses: An In-depth look at the Signals and Cues between Horses and their Handlers*

- ➢ *Walking with Horses: The Eight Leading Positions*

- ➢ *How to Create Good Horse Training Plans: The Art of Thin-Slicing*

If you prefer e-books but don't have a Kindle reader, Amazon has a free Kindle reader which can be downloaded to any computer, tablet or smartphone.

You can find the books by putting my name (Hertha James) into the Amazon search engine.

Table of Contents

Other Books   4

The Author   8

This Book Includes Free YouTube Links   9

Preface   11

Short Glossary   15

Chapter 1

Introduction   19

Saying Yes to 26 Questions   19

Overview of The Eight Exercises   25

The Fear Factor   32

    How Horses Deal with a Fearful Situation   33

    Anxiety and Fear Expression in Horses   35

    Risk Radar   36

The Responsibility of Care   37

Using Food for Motivation and Reward   41

Chapter 2

Handler Skills   47

    Reading Horse Body Language   47

        A: Signs of a horse in a state of relaxation   47

        B: Signs of a horse releasing tension   48

        C: Signs of Excitement   48

        D: Signs of a horse expressing annoyance or pain   49

        E: Signs of anxiety or fear-based stress   49

        F: Signs of a horse acting in self-defense   50

    Ears in Detail   50

Energy Management   52
   How we affect a horse   52
   How we enable relaxation   53
Signals   54
Handling Body Extensions: The Swishies   56
Reinforcement   58
Emotional Neutrality   60
How Long will it Take?   63

Skills Summary   67

Chapter 3
Communicating Zero Intent   71
Exercise 1: Quiet Sharing of Time and Space   71

Chapter 4
Zero Intent While the Handler is in Motion   83
Exercise 2: Active Sharing of Time and Space   84
   The Shy, Anxious, Flighty or Suspicious Horse   86
   The Intimidating Horse   87
Exercise 3: Greet & Go   89
   The Greet & Go Process   94

Chapter 5
Becoming the CEO   99
   Exercise 4: Claiming the Spot   100
   Exercise 5: Watchfulness   109
Key Points   119

Chapter 6
Moving Together   125
   Exercise 6: Guiding from Behind   125
   Exercise 7: Shadow Me   136

Exercise 8: The Boomerang Frolic   143

Chapter 7

Summary of the Eight Exercises   153

   1. Quiet Sharing of Time and Space   154

   2. Active Sharing of Time and Space   155

   3. Greet & Go   156

   4. Claiming the Spot   158

   5. Watchfulness   160

   6. Guiding from Behind   161

   7. Shadow Me   162

   8. Boomerang Frolic   164

Conclusion   165

Appendix 1:   Starting Clicker Training

   Materials: Gear Checklist   167

     Two Extra Points   170

   Method   171

     1. Simulation: Giving Meaning to the Click   171

     2. With the Horse   172

   Conclusion   179

Appendix 2:   List of YouTube Video Clips

   HorseGym with Boots Series   183

   Thin-Slicing Examples   186

   Free-Shaping Examples   187

Reference List   188

The Author

Hertha James grew up in Calgary just east of the Rocky Mountains. Her lifelong passion for horses began at age six with a ride on a big black horse. Animals of all kinds continue to be a constant part of her work and leisure.

Hertha's career with animals began with a zoology degree and included working as a zookeeper in Calgary and Wellington, New Zealand, as well as handling wild and exotic species for movie parts. Her animal experiences stood her in good stead when she changed careers to become a high school teacher of science and biology.

Hertha's other passion, creating teaching and learning resources, grew from her experience as a teacher.

Teaching science to teenagers for 23 years honed her ability to structure information clearly. It taught her how to build new knowledge in small steps and integrate it with the information and beliefs already held by her students.

Hertha applies the same successful strategy to teaching horses and their handlers. She has proved that horse training goals can be reached when valid starting points are based on gentle experimentation and good planning.

Acknowledgements

In this amazing digital world, as we cruise via the Internet, ideas come from everywhere. But for this work, I would like to especially acknowledge ideas put forward by Karen Pryor, Dr. Robert Miller, Gawani Pony Boy, Carolyn Resnick, Cynthia Royal and Farah DeJohnette.

This book was suggested by Lois Shaw in Canada and made better with the help of Bridget Evans in New Zealand. Thank you to Colleen Spence for her superb copy editing and Larry Metcalf whose input always improves my work. It is quite an international affair.

This Book Includes Free YouTube Links

Find my YouTube channel with a search for *Hertha Muddyhorse*. See Appendix 2 for a comprehensive list of all the clips available. Relevant video clips are mentioned throughout the book.

These two playlists are the key ones that relate to the ideas in this book:

1. <u>HorseGym with Boots</u>: Clips numbered 75-82 inclusive. These are the newest Universal Horse Language clips. For example, if you would like to view clip #76, simply put "*#76 HorseGym with Boots*" into the YouTube search engine and it should take you there. Each clip is identified by its number.

2. <u>Universal Horse Language</u>: This playlist contains older clips demonstrating the various exercises. The exercises are numbered 1-8. Scroll through the playlist to find the clips you want. I originally called these exercises: *Horse Herd Harmonics*, which will appear on some of the clips.

Other playlists that you may find helpful are:
<u>Free-Shaping</u>: These clips only have names. To find one, click on the playlist name and scroll down to find the title that you want.
<u>Thin-Slicing</u>: These clips only have names. To find one, click on the playlist name and scroll down to find the title that you want.

Preface

The purpose of the Universal Horse Language program is to set up comprehensive communication channels between a person and their own special horse or horses. The program is achieved when the person feels perfectly safe with the horse, and the horse feels perfectly safe with the handler. They understand each other. There are two main reasons why I felt compelled to write this book.

First Reason

There is a significant turnover of people who take up horses and then give them up again. This suggests that there are many people who acquire a horse without knowing much about them. The unfortunate outcome for many horses is that they go through a succession of owners.

When a horse and handler first meet, both are faced with an unknown quantity. If we breed and raise a foal ourselves, we'll know a lot about it. If we are well acquainted with the horse-breeding facility from which we acquire a horse, we may have a good idea about how the horse was fed and handled. The horse, of course, has no way of knowing anything about us. He has to learn to read the intentions of every human he meets from scratch.

If the horse comes from a background unknown to us, anything is possible. The horse may have been treated kindly, harshly or with inconsistency anywhere along the kindness-harshness continuum. The horse may be well adjusted to living with people or he may be an emotional wreck. The horse may view people with benign interest or be terrified about people and what they might do.

Learning and using the Universal Horse Language exercises gives both the horse and the handler time and opportunity to get to know each other initially, or to expand an existing relationship. A horse who is shut down emotionally and mentally in order to survive, will need much longer, and more empathy from his new handler, to gain a sense of calmness, to understand his new situation, and to engage with the handler willingly.

There is a fair amount of trauma involved when a horse is removed from the home he knows and abruptly deposited into another place. Time to adjust can be as long as two years for some sensitive-natured horses. Even the most chilled out horse needs about three months to feel 'at home' in a new, kind, horse-centered situation. In some environments, a horse may never get to feel at home and able to relax.

The first priority of good teaching and learning is relaxation of both the teacher and the student. That's why the first Universal Horse Language exercise, *Quiet Sharing of Time and Space* is the crucial exercise. Once the horse is able to accept our presence in his environment in a quiet, companionable way, we can gradually introduce the other seven exercises one at a time. Each exercise builds on the one before it.

Using Universal Horse Language gives us a way of assessing our horse because we work through the exercises gradually as the horse shows us he is ready to do more. The time frame is flexible and there are no time limits. Five of the exercises become part of our regular repertoire. There are developmental exercises that we use to establish the two-way relationship, then fade out when we no longer need them because the horse's response has become a habit.

Second Reason

My second reason for wanting to write this book is the increasing popularity of using reward or positive reinforcement with horses. This is usually called clicker training. Like the rest of us, horses prefer to work for a reward rather than to avoid pressure. I've worked with clicker training for many years and can't imagine being with a horse without using it.

Appendix 1 outlines a way you can experiment with clicker training to see if you would like to incorporate it into the way you interact with your horses. Equine clicker training is a wonderful way forward for all horse trainers, but there are some cautions to be taken.

The size and quickness of horses means that there is always a danger of being hurt. Even the most placid, experienced horse can be startled into instant action. Even the smallest pony can kick in your kneecap.

Clicker training coaches suggest starting with the horse behind a fence or gate to set the foundation for safe food delivery by the handler and polite food retrieval by the horse. But at some point, in order not to bore the horse to death, we want to use clicker training with the horse in active mode. To do that, we have to feel totally safe in the horse's presence, and the horse has to feel totally safe in our presence.

The safest horse is a horse at liberty in an area where he can freely move far enough away to feel safe. That is the starting point for this Universal Horse Language program. It doesn't matter whether your horse prefers to graze at your feet as you sit in a chair, or whether he watches you from the furthers corner of its enclosure.

Two situations arise when we begin interact actively with our horse. Firstly, if the handler is new to horses, he or she will not have the background experience to deal with complex, often unexpected situations that will inevitably arise.

Secondly, A horse needs basic training or education to a level, that allows him to:

- feel relaxed around people
- accept being in small spaces
- respond rather than react to rope or rein pressure
- respond rather than react to stick pressure indicating that he needs to move away
- respond rather than react to the many domestic horse situations that will arise.

Clicker training, by itself, will not give the horse the skills he needs to respond to the pressure he may face. Pressures such as the behavior of vets, farriers or barefoot trimmers, horse transporters, stable workers and visitors if the horse is boarded at a facility. To be fair to our horse, we need to teach him about some of the basic routines used by other people. At the same time, of course, we can introduce the idea of clicker training to vets and farriers and horse transporters and stable workers.

If the horse has inadequate education about how to survive in captivity, and the handler is new to horses, the combination can become tricky and dangerous. The equine clicker training forums on the Internet throw up interesting stories of people who are determined to use only clicker training but come unstuck when faced with the unusual.

The purpose of the Universal Horse Language exercises is to lay the foundation for a safe two-way relationship between a handler and his or her horse. The kindly people who believe that carrying two sticks to enlarge their personal bubble is animal cruelty, may come to realize that the only purpose of the sticks is to allow our gestures to be more horse-like.

The people who believe it is okay to hit horses with sticks will hopefully come to realize that disturbing the air with two swishy twigs is all the message that most horses need to let them know that we would like them to move away.

Universal Horse Language is a program for people to become more horse-like. While we take the time to do this, the horse has time to get to know us better. Together, the person and horse work out their two-way communication system. The horse knows the language already. The person's challenge is to become consistent in their approach to the horse. It all happens on the ground with the horse at liberty in a roomy area.

Short Glossary

Body Extensions: general name for the sticks, whips, wands, reeds, pointers, strings, ropes, halters, reins, bridles, saddles and harnesses that people use with horses. (See also, Swishies.)

Clicker Training: general name for training using a 'mark and reward' system. We can use a mechanical clicker, a tongue click, a special word or any special sound to 'mark' the exact moment that the horse is doing what we want. The marker sound is immediately followed by a small food treat.

Click&treat: the click marks the exact behavior we would like. The treat follows immediately after the click. The horse will seek to repeat the behavior that produced the click followed by the treat. This dynamic is also called the 'mark and reward' system.

Developmental Exercises: three of the eight Universal Horse Language exercises are used to establish an understanding with the horse. Once the understanding is reached, there is no need to repeat the exercises unless we occasionally want to refresh them. They include, *Active Sharing of Time and Space, Claiming the Spot,* and *Watchfulness*. The other five exercises become activities that we can use any time.

Emotional Neutrality: the ability to stay calm and not buy into any upset that the horse or people around us are showing. Horses are highly tuned-in to the emotional state of other horses and people nearby. If we can remain calm, the horse is able to connect to our calmness. If we are nervous, afraid or fearful, the horse has no reason to feel comfortable with what we are asking him to do.

Etiquette: ways of behaving between members of a group that are accepted by all members of the group. Horse etiquette includes horses lower in the social order giving way to horses higher in the social order. It also includes sending messages starting with minimal energy (flick of an ear or a focused look) and increasing energy into a snaking neck, and finally a bite, if the lower order horse does not comply quickly enough. A look might be followed by a movement of the hind end followed by a raised hind leg followed by a kick. Other aspects of equine etiquette include respect for each other's personal space and alerting each other to possible danger.

Realistic Goals: something which can be achieved to a reasonable standard in a relatively short time. By confidently achieving small goals we gain the confidence and motivation to try something new. If a goal is too difficult and takes a long time to achieve, it is not realistic. We never reach the positive feeling of completion and our motivation decreases.

Release Reinforcement (-R): removing signal pressure (which might be very light) or removing discomfort caused by putting pressure on the horse. It is also called *negative reinforcement*. **Note** however that 'negative' is not used in the sense of being bad. It is used in the mathematical sense of subtracting something (i.e. the signal pressure we have applied) from a situation. This is the most common type of reinforcement used by horse trainers.

Reward Reinforcement (+R): when the horse complies with a request, we highlight the moment with a marker signal and promptly deliver a treat. (See *Click&treat* above.) The treat must be something the horse loves to receive, usually a tasty morsel.

It is also often called *positive reinforcement*. **Note** that the term 'positive' is used in the mathematical sense of adding something to the situation, in this case a marker sound and a treat.

Many people think, incorrectly, that the removal of their signal pressure is the reward and therefore it is positive reinforcement. Actually, the release of the pressure is negative reinforcement because the pressure has been removed.

This misunderstanding has led to a great deal of confusion for people trying to do their best with their horses.

Signal pressure: whenever we show up and want the horse to do things with us, we are exerting signal pressure. The pressure can become an extremely light message of communication once the horse understands what we want.

In some circumstances, the pressure will be more intense if we have to clarify a message or if safety is our first concern.

Thin-slicing: cutting a whole task into its smallest teachable (clickable) parts so we can teach the horse in a way that allows him to be continually successful.

Swishies: flexible body extensions that we can use to disturb the air between us and the horse, either to expand our personal bubble or to cause the horse to move. They can be dressage whips or something like long willow twigs. Their purpose is to make our body more horse-like by giving us more reach. We use them to assert ourselves, **not** as aggressive or offensive weapons. Used consistently and correctly, horses see them as a natural extension of our strange, upright bodies.

Thresholds: a threshold is the point at which we begin to feel uncomfortable. While we are 'within threshold' we are in our comfort zone. Our heart rate and breathing rate are normal and we feel at ease. As we approach a threshold, we begin to feel uneasy. When we go 'over threshold', we are out of our comfort zone and feel nervous tension such as butterflies in the stomach, sweating, faster breathing and heartrate, and nausea. Anxiety, nervousness and panic increase if we are forced to remain beyond our normal threshold for a long time. The same applies to horses.

Universal Horse Language: eight exercises that allow people to communicate in ways that resemble horse communication as closely as possible. The exercises are done with the horse at liberty in a roomy enclosure.

Chapter 1

Introduction

The eight exercises that make up Universal Horse Language can be done alongside anything else you are doing with your horse. For easy reading, I'll refer to horses as he or him unless writing about a specific mare.

The safest horse is a horse that is not constrained. A horse free to move and make choices will feel safer than a horse tied or confined in a small space. A horse that feels safe is able to observe, think and make choices that enable him to get along with the least stress possible.

When we use Universal Horse Language, we enable the horse to say, "Yes, I understand your body language and I'm prepared to listen to you." When we eventually add halter and rope or bridle and reins, the horse will already know a great deal about us and how we communicate.

Saying Yes to 26 Questions

By learning Universal Horse Language, you will be able to say yes to the following questions without the need to use a rope to influence the horse.
1. Can I make the time to sit and read or meditate or just 'be', either outside my horse's enclosure or inside a roomy area with my horse?
2. Can I tell whether my horse is fearful, curious and friendly, or pushy and intimidating?
3. Can I attract my cautious horse with carrots under my chair?
4. Can I protect my personal bubble from my pushy or over-friendly horse?

5. Can I decide when to move my chair or ask my horse to step back?
6. Can I wander around quietly in our shared area and have my horse remain unconcerned?
7. Can I wander around relaxed but swishing my swishies and the horse remains unconcerned?
8. Can I (every day and often) approach the horse from the front, offer my outstretched hand, allow the horse to close the distance to touch my hand, then walk away?
9. Can I move my horse off his hay pile or grazing spot using my body language amplified by my swishies if necessary?
10. Can I move my horse off his hay pile or grazing spot using only my body language?
11. Can I move into my horse's rear blind spot when he is eating and tell whether he is watching me or not?
12. If I'm in his rear blind spot and he is not watching, can I move him off the hay and keep him away until he faces me politely at which point can I invite him back to the food?
13. Can I ask my horse to walk away from me and keep moving until I stop?
14. Can I ask my horse to move away from me, keep him moving and influence his direction until I stop?
15. Can I get my horse to stop when I ask for a "Whoa"?
16. Can I indicate to the horse that I'd like him to walk beside me?
17. Can I influence the horse to go left or right as we walk along together side-by-side?
18. Can I influence the horse to keep walking with me, slow as I slow and speed up as I speed up?
19. Can I influence the horse to jog with me?
20. Can I influence the horse to walk, jog and halt with me?
21. Can I influence the horse to back up with me?

22. Can I tell if my horse might be in the mood to play?
23. Do I know ways of inviting my horse to play or frolic so he is encouraged to want to interact with me?
24. Can I influence the horse to move away from me at a trot?
25. Can I influence the horse to move away from me at a canter?
26. Can I influence the horse to return to me?

Universal Horse Language is the body language used by horses to communicate with each other. Animals that live in groups have developed systems that allow them to live together in relative harmony even though they all have the same needs from their environment.

Horses in a group compete for access to best grazing, shade, shelter, safest water. Stallions in a natural situation compete for mares. The communication system that allows the group to live together has to be powerful enough to override their daily competition for resources. The more limited the resources, the stronger the competition.

More and more people are spending time observing groups of horses in natural or near-natural environments and writing about their experiences and the knowledge they have gained. There appear to be significant differences between the herd behavior of feral horses and the group behavior of domestic horses put together into paddocks. Feral horses are free to choose their own companions. They can move between groups. The rigors of daily life mean that they don't have the pent-up energy and frustrations suffered by many domestic horses.

Becoming familiar with such work enables more and more horse owners to become aware of the group dynamics that orchestrate the life of horses, and to use this knowledge to communicate more clearly with their horses.

A group of horses may appear peaceful but the peace is maintained through a carefully orchestrated social order. The life of a horse living in a group is prescribed to some extent by the will of the horses above him in the social order. He will yield position to these horses. As well as watching out for the horses to which he gives way, a horse is aware of which horses in the group yield to him. These behaviors are exaggerated when food resources are in short supply.

Some horses are easy-going while others seem to have a strong instinct to rise in the social order. When times are good the easy-going horses will thrive because they use up little energy jockeying for social position. When times are hard, the social climbers will get the best deal because they have more access to resources in the depths of winter and during dry summers.

This jockeying for social position has led to the development of a sophisticated set of equine body language which I've called Universal Horse Language. Horses everywhere understand it. In your relationship with a horse, you need to be sure that he will move away at your request – not with fear, but because he understands your intent just like he understands the intent of other horses in his group.

Universal Horse Language is something horses know already. The person is the one doing the learning in this situation. The horse will notice when his person's body language becomes consistent and starts to make sense. He will respond accordingly.

Young or inexperienced horses should ideally be educated slowly in a program that builds confidence with each little step. Exactly the same applies to teaching horsemanship to a person. As soon as confidence is lost in either the horse or the person, the ability to learn effectively and thoughtfully goes out the window.

When we lose confidence, we become reactive rather than responsive. The first lesson we all need to learn well is how to rewind a fraught situation and regain relaxation for both parties so they can start again. This is called a reset. It requires emotional neutrality.

People who are talented naturals with horses can have the greatest difficulty teaching people new to horses because they have no concept of how much a human student doesn't yet know and can't yet see. They may have difficulty realizing that they have to minutely break down and explain things that seem obvious to them.

A new wave of trainers realizes that they must be people trainers at the same time as horse trainers. The horse and its owner or handler have to be treated as a unit or a partnership. The challenge is for each horse and handler to learn to communicate with each other. Home study materials such as this book and accompanying YouTube video clips can be helpful. Learning Universal Horse Language is a way to build or strengthen a bond of understanding between a horse and his handler.

A keen horse person will strive to appreciate a horse's view of the world. Horses have acute senses that are tuned to every nuance and change in their environment. It is what was demanded by the harsh habitat of the dry grasslands on which horses evolved.

Horses are a prey species with flight response uppermost in their psyche. They are hard-wired genetically to run first and ask questions second. Horses are smart about learning what might be a threat, what is harmless and where the food might be as the seasons change.

For wild horses, finding enough food is their main concern for much of the year. Their life revolves around finding food and water, avoiding predators, reproduction and the daily soap opera of herd dynamics to decide who gets the best grass, the nicest shade, the first drink - if any of these are in short supply.

We may have removed these stress points from our domestic horses' lives but their responses are still the instinctive responses that enabled the species to survive millions of years in tough environments. Horses are keen observers, learn quickly and have excellent memories.

Humans have another layer of intelligence. We can figure things out logically and plan ahead, therefore people have the ability to learn to read horse body language and to use a form of it to communicate, giving horses a better chance at understanding what we would like them to do.

Learning and using Universal Horse Language helps us gain a better understanding of the emotional, mental and physical aspects of our horses. Once people understand the attitude and techniques required to be effective with Universal Horse

Language, they are able to behave less like a person and more like a horse.

The eight exercises in this program provide information to guide you through learning the etiquette that allows a group of horses to function as a successful unit. The more we can emulate this natural horse etiquette, the safer we will be and the more fun we can have.

Horses are not like motorbikes that you send to the repair shop and get them back fixed. Horses are more like children. They need a teacher they trust. They need regular, consistent education via enjoyable activities that increase in complexity as they get older and smarter. They need to be exposed to many situations to give them opportunities to become bolder about the strange things we ask and expect them to do.

Like children, each horse will have his own timeline for learning something new. Respecting the horse's timeline helps build lifelong confidence because the horse has time to put new learning into deep memory.

Some horses have never had the opportunity to live in a group of horses. They may never have learned polite group behavior as youngsters through living freely with other horses. They may have learned to intimidate people with tactics involving their size and strength. Correctly carried out, the Universal Horse Language exercises can help such a horse develop horse etiquette. You will be teaching him his relative position in your group of two in a language that he can understand.

A horse will accept his position because you calmly act and respond to him like another horse higher in his social order. Once you understand how these exercises hang together and once you are fluid in your movements, it is relatively easy to apply them to any horse or use them when you are among a group of horses.

Establishing your position may briefly require considerable energy if you are dealing with a confident horse who has learned ways to push people around. At the other extreme, establishing your position as a companion with an anxious, shy or terrified horse may need weeks of quiet, low-key interaction.

As you consistently behave like a senior horse, your horse will accept your position as higher in the social order. As your relationship becomes more established, it will take less energy to have him accept your suggestions. Some horses are confident and enjoy testing boundaries on a regular basis. At the other end of the spectrum are horses who remain cautious their whole lifetime. It will be harder to win their enduring trust.

Knowing the character type of our horse helps us make better decisions. My book, *How to Create Good Horse Training Plans,* has a section about horse character types.

Overview of The Eight Exercises

For the horse, there is a huge difference between a person building a relationship using the Universal Horse Language approach and a person using the restriction of ropes and small pens. By learning and using the natural language of a horse, we enter his world rather than drag him into ours. We learn to influence the horse in ways that he easily understands.

The first exercise, *Quiet Sharing of Time and Space* establishes or strengthens the basic bond between you and the horse. Just as we make human friends by spending time with them, so you and the horse can only get well acquainted by spending time and space together on a regular basis.

The only expectation during *Quiet Sharing of Time and Space* is politeness. We can carry on doing this exercise with our horse for as long as we have him.

Figure 1: Quiet Sharing of Time and Space: Bridget and Boots are enjoying quiet time together. The time can be as short or long as fits into your daily life. We want the space to be somewhere the horse is relaxed.

The second exercise, *Active Sharing of Time and Space*, allows the horse to get comfortable with you moving around his area minding your own business. We are present in the horse's home like another horse would be present. This is a developmental exercise that we don't do forever.

Figure 2: Active Sharing of Time and Space: Bridget is walking in the paddock in a relaxed manner in the same way as another horse would move around the paddock.

In Figure 2, Bridget is gently moving her swishies right and left across the front of her body as she walks along. If she accidentally enters Boots' personal space bubble, she will immediately move further away.

The third exercise, *Greet & Go,* lays the foundation of a lifelong polite way to greet each other without the expectation of further interaction. This exercise becomes something we do every time we meet up with a horse.

Figure 3: Greet & Go: Bridget holds out her hand and allows the horse to close the last two inches of space to put his nose on her hand. Then she goes back to doing whatever she was doing. This is a small but very powerful exercise we learn to use every time we meet up with a horse.

The fourth exercise, *Claiming the Spot,* allows you to rise in the social order. By behaving like a horse higher in the social order, you are able to keep yourself safe as well as encourage the horse's willingness to follow your suggestions. This is a developmental exercise we use to build a mutual understanding.

Figure 4: Claiming the Spot: Bridget has used just enough energy to cause Boots to move off another pile of hay.

The fifth exercise, *Watchfulness*, builds the horse's awareness of where you are and what you are doing. It is a developmental exercise that you use to build a mutual understanding. Once the horse is convinced that it is in his best interests to keep an eye on you, it only needs to be used occasionally to check that his watchfulness is still there.

Figure 5: Watchfulness: As soon as we can see our horse, he can see us. If we have an established relationship, the horses will be curious about our intent.

The sixth exercise, *Guiding from Behind*, makes the horse comfortable with the idea that we will follow behind him, first to encourage his movement and eventually to build a "Whoa" voice signal. Horses often move each other by hazing from behind.

Guiding from Behind is what we do when we ride, so this exercise is a super foundation for riding or driving.

Figure 6: Guiding from Behind: When the horse moves off willingly and halts willingly at signals from behind, we have taught him the prerequisites for riding or driving without needing ropes and reins.

If you build the *Guiding from Behind* communication on the ground with the horse at liberty, it will be there for you when you ride as long as you don't suddenly turn predatory when you mount up. It is quite common for people to get skilled with their horse on the ground, but then suddenly expect way too much of the horse when they get on his back.

Figure 7: Riding is simply a form of Guiding from Behind.

Novice or occasional riders need time to develop an independent seat and confidence at all the gaits. The horse's learning timeline needs to be respected but the person's timeline requires equal attention.

The seventh exercise, *Shadow Me*, develops the habit of walking together side-by-side. This is the leading positon we use most of the time in our daily care and management of our horses.

Figure 8: Shadow Me: Bridget and Smoky walking together.

The eighth exercise, the *Boomerang Frolic*, sets up opportunities to send the horse away from us and to invite him back. It might seem counter-intuitive, but each time we break our close connection, we have another opportunity to call the horse back to us and re-establish the connection.

Figure 9: Boomerang Frolic: I've sent Boots away and now I'm stepping backwards to signal to her that she can come back in. She worried about being sent away at first, but now it is a game we both understand.

Asking how long it takes to establish a polite, positive, active relationship with a particular horse is a bit like asking, "How long is a piece of string?" There is no formula. It will depend on:

- the nature of your existing relationship
- your level of empathy
- your experience with horses
- the horse's responses based on his innate characteristics, environment, state of health, spirit and previous experiences with people.

The coming chapters look at each of the eight Universal Horse Language exercises in detail.

The Fear Factor

It's entirely reasonable to have an element of fear when we are around horses. Even the smallest pony's kick can split open someone's skull or destroy a kneecap. Bigger horses are a hazard due to their sheer size and weight. Even the most polite and well-mannered horse can suddenly be startled and unintentionally hurt a person.

Some domestic horses have experienced people in a way that induces distress and unease. Some horses have learned that the best defense to perceived predator-like actions by humans is a good offense. They have learned that putting ears back and lunging at people keeps unwanted attention away.

Quite often these sorts of behaviors are interpreted by people as a horse challenging them or showing disrespect. When in reality, the horse is simply being a horse and responding in the only way he can if he is kept for long hours in a tiny enclosure where he is bored stiff. When he is taken out for groundwork or riding, he is usually constantly constrained with ropes and reins. Besides avoiding the pain of saddles, whips and spurs, the only thing of importance in his life is when his next meal is coming.

For an animal adapted to live in family groups on the open range with a great deal of moving over 24 hours, being kept in isolation in tiny spaces must be an especially poignant punishment. Many people are so used to seeing horses suffer physiological and emotional distress as a result of the way they are kept, they have arrogantly coined the term 'stable vices', as if it is somehow the horse's fault.

A little bit of fear on our part leads to a healthy respect for a horse's size and potential to hurt us and himself. It motivates us to learn more about how horses live naturally and makes us seek better ways to educate our horse so he can calmly do the things we would like him to do.

On the other hand, a lot of fear often causes us to become aggressive with a horse whose behavior scares us. Fear makes us forget that the horse has not chosen to be contained and restrained. That is all our doing.

If a horse is using body language so strong that we fear for our safety, that horse has not been educated so he can have positive interactions with people. The fault lies with the people, not the horse.

Horses don't understand punishment. They interpret aggressive and violent action by people as the behavior of a predator attempting to capture, corner and eat them.

We put the horse in a position of captivity and expect him to get used to all sorts of things he would never encounter in the wild. When we use ropes and small pens, we have removed the horse's primary way of feeling safe again, which is the ability to move away and re-assess a situation.

How Horses Deal with a Fearful Situation

Horses have their own unique way of dealing with situations that evoke their fear response. If we set up a spooky object in the horses' home area while they are not there, we can observe their reactions when they return and first see the spooky thing.

Their bodies instantly switch into high alert. If the item is spooky enough, they move away from it until they feel safe enough to turn, face it, and reconsider.

If the spooky object does not give chase, the bolder horses approach a little way, then retreat again. Gradually, if the unknown object stays quiet, each approach gets closer to the object and each retreat is shorter.

If nothing happens to spook the horses again, the boldest horse eventually puts his whiskers on the spooky object or he may check it out by pawing.

If we watch closely, we can see the moment a horse makes the decision that he can relax with a new object. His body relaxes, his head comes down, he may lick and chew, and he returns to grazing, resting, or his social engagements.

Other horses in the group do a similar exploration or they accept the decision of the bolder horse and relax when they relax.

Horses naturally thin-slice the task of confidence-building about anything unusual in their environment. Here is a summary of the way horses naturally deal with a fear response.

1. Retreat to a distance which allows them to feel safe enough to stop, turn and reconsider.
2. Advance to the edge of their comfort zone and observe the spooky object.
3. If nothing happens to reignite their flight response, their comfort zone expands and they advance a bit more.
4. Repeat 3 until they are comfortable enough to put their nose or foot on the object to check it out.
5. Make a decision. The horses will decide that there is danger and move away or they may decide that there is no danger and accept the presence of the unusual new item.
6. Carry on with everyday life; grazing, browsing, social interactions and resting.

Most training systems don't allow the horse to move far enough away or give him the time he needs to make decisions about whether something is dangerous or harmless. By starting or re-creating our relationship using the eight exercises of Universal Horse Language, we do two things.

1. Preserve the horse's dignity and give him time to learn. He can move away or choose to link up with us.
2. Build a strong safety factor into the relationship. The key to being with horses is to understand how to be assertive when the need arises. We have to know how to be assertive, like another herd member higher in the social order, <u>without</u> being aggressive.

Anxiety and Fear Expression in Horses

It's important that we learn to recognize the body language of horses who are anxious or afraid. Things to look for include:
- whole body tension
- high head
- staring eyes
- stiff ears
- tight lips
- tightly clamped tail; J-shaped tail if fear is extreme
- desire to move feet away from the situation – always a first response and why most people use ropes and small pens
- the dropped head of a horse that has gone internal – a sort of non-blinking paralysis called catalepsy.

Horses acting in self-defense will choose to leave our presence, but if that is not possible they may:
- run endless circles if they are in a round pen
- bite
- strike with a front leg
- turn the hindquarters toward the source of fear
- kick with one or both hind legs
- charge
- buck if there is pain from saddle and/or the rider
- rear if forward movement is blocked.

When a horse is shut down, shows anxiety, shows fear or engages in self-defense actions, we have to look to ourselves and change what we are doing and how we are managing the horse's daily life.

Risk Radar

Around horses, our risk management radar must be constantly turned on. It helps if we:
- try to avoid making assumptions
- check for hazards and deal with them
- realize that temperature, wind, other horses, other people, new places, something moved from where it was before, are all highly significant to a horse and will influence his behavior
- learn to read our horse from moment to moment.
- don't expect our horse to necessarily act the same way today as he did yesterday.

Very anxious, shy, or frightened horses may also find it easier to approach if you begin interaction on the other side of a fence.

Horses learn in the same way as we do. It takes an average of seven confident repetitions before we can expect our mammal brains to have created a strong enough chemical pathway for that memory to remain intact. Some things will be learned more quickly; other things will take much longer. Trauma or excitement often result in single episode learning, creating a memory (good or bad) which seems to be seared into the brain.

Continuity is important. The more often you can repeat an individual learning task in short sessions over a day and then over several days, tailing off into every second day and then occasionally, the stronger that task will remain as part of your horse's permanent repertoire. After all, we don't send our children to school occasionally and expect them to pass the exams. If you can only play with your horse occasionally, you will need to adjust your expectations accordingly.

Even so, playing with the Universal Horse Language exercises when you can fit them into a busy life is much better than not doing them at all. Many people have found significant changes in their horses from what seems like just a small change in their own behavior around their horse.

We have to use the environments we have available and adapt them to our purpose. Carefully setting up the requirements for each exercise will help ensure success.

Doing these processes with a new horse, will obviously be different from doing them with a horse with whom you already have an established relationship. Doing them with a horse who is fearful around people will be completely different to doing them with a horse who views people kindly.

The Responsibility of Care

Horses are hard-wired to recognize a predator and respond by flight, or if cornered, fight. Some domestic horses, if overwhelmed by stimuli and knowing they cannot physically leave a situation, cope by hiding inside themselves. It is a sort of playing dead like the frozen immobility of a newborn fawn or hare. This is called a cataleptic state.

Often, seemingly quiet horses are in reality dwelling in a place of deep, silent, anxiety. Sometimes they suddenly explode out of this internal place in fighting mode. Not recognizing the fearfully withdrawn horse can lead to dangerous situations.

Many other horses have simply learned to shut down their feelings and comply with human requests or demands because there is no choice. Horses that can't learn to shut down and comply often have a past but not much of a future.

Domestic Horses Need Specific Life Skills

Learning Universal Horse Language allows us to help the horse develop the essential life skills he needs to live more comfortably in a human-regulated environment. A horse's behavior links directly to the behavior of his companion person. It takes a split second for a horse to read our fear or our confidence, our intent or our lack of purpose.

Universal Horse Language helps people develop confident, safer horses by becoming confident and safe themselves. The eight exercises teach the handler that he or she can move the horse safely in a variety of situations. The eight exercises, done well, teach the horse that the handler knows Universal Horse Language. Once both you and your horse feel safe and confident together, there is no end to the fun you can have.

When we gain control of ourselves, the horse will follow. Horses, like people, prefer fair and confident companions. The eight exercises in this book are designed to help guide people toward becoming such a companion.

Thin-Slicing is the Key

Mastery learning involves breaking a big task into its tiniest component parts and teaching each one separately. The parts are then gradually strung together. This is a most effective learning system, both for people and for horses. Planning on paper is important. It allows you to get your head around exactly what you want to accomplish. My book, *How to Create Good Horse Training Plans*, looks at the planning process in detail.

Once you have decided how to slice up an overall task, you put the slices into an order that seems logical to you. You and the horse master the first slice before you work with the second one. Then you join the two together and begin working on the third slice. If at any point the training wavers (which it will) you go back to the slice that is still solid for both of you and start again from there.

I've found that the 'going back' part is the hardest for many people. We expect that if the horse did it yesterday, he should also do it today, tomorrow or a week later. The fastest way forward is always going back to a point of confidence every time confidence is lost.

Each of the Universal Horse Language Exercises builds on the exercise before it, so it is important to do them in order. Once you and the horse know how all the exercises work, five of them can be incorporated into your regular interactions. Once a horse truly understands a task and we have consistently practiced it enough to put it into deep memory, the horse will not forget.

Figure 10: Since first learning to smile, Boots has had lots of opportunity to practice and be rewarded for her smile. Anytime I ask, "Gotta smile?" she knows immediately what I mean. The voice signal and action are in her deep, long-term memory.

If we consider our responsibility of care seriously, we will realize that the more we understand about the nature of horses, the better deal we can give them when they are forced to live as captive domestic animals.

Some of the variables to consider when we set up a training program include:
- horse's innate character type
- person's personality
- horse's previous experiences
- person's previous experiences
- person's knowledge of the natural behavior and needs of horses
- person's confidence around horses
- horse's confidence around people

- person's goals with the horse
- how the horse is kept
- how much time the person can devote to the horse
- strength of the current two-way communication between horse and person

The quality of a training program will also be affected by the willingness of the person to:

- suspend judgment of new ideas until they are tried out
- gain more knowledge from a variety of sources
- move out of their comfort zone
- acknowledge their own thresholds and those of the horse
- observe, remember, compare
- experiment
- get it wrong and try again
- accept the mental state of not knowing something yet
- overcome frustration, annoyance and fear
- allow sufficient time and steady practice for new behaviors to become ho-hum — both the person's and the horse's new behaviors.

'Responsibility of care' is more than just the physical health of our horse. We also have to concern ourselves with his emotional and intellectual welfare. By learning and using Universal Horse Language, we can make the horse secure about his place in our relationship. Most of the time, the handler will suggest what happens next and the horse complies. Occasionally, the horse will make a suggestion that the handler goes along with. Some training systems, such as www.Intrinzen.horse, make a fine art out of free-shaping exuberant movements using only reward reinforcement.

Horses thrive on attention and new learning as long as the new experiences are developed with sensitivity to the nature and previous experiences of the specific horse.

Using Food for Motivation and Reward

The range of opinions about using food as part of training is extremely interesting. There are people who never use treats or allow their horses to graze or nibble when they are riding. There are some horses who are too afraid to eat in the company of their person.

Clicker training, on the other hand, feeds a treat with every click until the horse understands the request and has learned a signal and responds to the signal consistently. At that point, when the horse has the new thing firmly in its repertoire, the click&treat can be used intermittently to support the horse's enthusiasm or refine the task further.

A few things about clicker training are often misunderstood by people who have not studied it and used it. The first thing the horse learns when we start clicker training is that mugging gets him nothing. The second thing taught is that a treat follows only if there was click (marker signal) first, and treats are taken politely by the horse.

The treats are the horse's wages for offering the response we want. We are paying for piecework. As the horse gets to understand the click&treat dynamic, we start to withhold the click to get a slightly longer wait or a few more good strides or picking up a cone rather than just sniffing it, or getting three feet on the pedestal rather than just two. In this manner, we build the behavior by tiny increments until it is where we ultimately want it. There are some great clips on You Tube if your interest is piqued. Search for *HorseGym with Boots*.

What is the horse's opinion about food? It pays to remember that horses evolved in Asian grasslands. Like feral horses nowadays, their main aim in life, besides avoiding predators and seeing off competitors, is to find enough calories to stay alive. The only easy time is probably during the spring growth season. Summer drought and winter snow make survival marginal. So, food is tops on a horse's list of priorities, especially the high calorie foods we often use for treats. Mare's milk is sweet, so horses also have a natural sweet tooth.

Many horses absolutely light up when food is brought into the learning equation. It will never be as important as safety, but for a horse that feels safe and is relaxed (i.e., not having an adrenalin rush and needing to release excess energy), food is usually number one.

Treats versus Bribes

Some people use a treat as a reward when the horse comes to them in the paddock or after it has cooperated with haltering. It is a powerful reinforcing agent. Treats can be a pre-date offering (bringing wine to dinner) or a post-date thanks (sending a thank-you box of chocolates).

Some people like to visit their horse with a treat as a friendly gesture, then go away again.

Some people add a treat to their 'pressure off' body language when the horse has done something especially well.

Some people use treats as an incentive. For example, getting a horse to explore a tarp, to cross a stream or puddle, to go through a narrow place. If a treat is in the trailer when the horse gets bold enough to go in, the treat acts as a reinforcement.

What's the difference between an incentive (or bribe) versus a reward or a bonus? A very good question. An incentive gives the horse a purpose or reason for doing something. A reward is offered after the behavior has occurred.

#74 HorseGym with Boots is a clip showing a trailer loading simulation. When I added a bowl with a few carrot strips to the front of the trailer simulation, Boots immediately stopped worrying about the high sides flapping in the wind because I had given her a reason to go into the strange, narrow space.

A bribe has a different feel to it than an incentive. Perhaps a bribe is more in the line of forcing a horse to do something specific because we want it to happen right now as opposed to setting it up as an incentive to help the horse learn something in his own time, e.g. a piece of apple on a tarp to encourage the horse to explore and step on the tarp.

Some people teach saddling by giving the horse his dinner as soon as he's saddled, then unsaddling again. Such sequences give the horse a positive feeling about the saddling experience that lives on after you no longer need to do the sequence because the horse is completely calm and accepting about the saddle.

Similarly, when first teaching a horse to wear a saddle in motion, or if striving to re-educate a saddle-sour horse, going for in-hand grazing sessions after saddling (which double as non-agenda time to some extent) creates a positive purpose for the horse. If no grazing is available, lead the horse to buckets of food or hay set out in a circuit. Procedures like this help to take the horse's mind off the saddle by giving him something positive to do and think about.

The same strategy can work when riding to help a reluctant, anxious, worried, or shut down horse to follow our suggestions more willingly. We can ride out to a patch of nice grass and allow dwell time with grazing. Then we can ride on to another nice grass spot and do the same. No grass? Put some piles of hay or buckets of food or pieces of apple/carrot in strategic places along your route. The horse will be impressed with the way you know where these yummy things are. This method can act as a powerful incentive.

When I first took my horse out in a trailer, I laid pieces of apple around the new venue before I asked her out of the trailer. Our first job on leaving the trailer was to find these apple pieces. It gave my horse something to do and it gave her a reason to follow my suggestions about where to go next.

Once the horse is comfortable with the process of getting saddled and ridden out (because he recognises a positive culinary purpose) the good feeling will remain even when we no longer need to put out the food or stop for grazing quite so often.

At that point we can carry our treat of choice and give him one whenever he does something well. We can mark the action with a tongue click or special sound, and follow it up with the treat. He might stop well, cross water well, do a nice smooth move that you've asked for or walk past a scary thing without spooking. You will find things to reward once you start carrying the treats and looking for things to reward.

The positive communication that is achieved by rewarding a good job has quite a different feel than going along looking for things to correct. Under which type of regime would you personally rather operate? Click&treat adds a wonderful positive dynamic because it makes what we want much clearer to the horse.

Some people use a treat, like apple sauce in a worming syringe, to get the horse to have a positive response to paste worming and oral medications.

When riding outside of arenas, grass and shrubbery can become the focus of our horse's attention. Interestingly, the easiest way I have found to teach a horse not to eat is to teach him when it is okay to eat. I ask for 'head up' and am ready to support my signal with a tap on the butt (making sure I stay well out of the kick zone) if the head is not up in a second or two. I prefer not to pull on the head. I want rope and rein signals to the head to remain light and directional. When the head comes up, I click&treat. When I ask for 'head down' the grass is the reward.

We practice this until it is well established. At first, I jump up and act all excited when I ask for 'heads up', as if there is a wolf on the horizon. Then, as we practice it regularly, I tone down my body language. The key is to stay totally consistent. Confident horses are often looking for that chink in our behavior that suggests we might not be up to standard today.

When I walk along the road with Boots, she knows the lush grass on either side is out of bounds unless I give the signal for 'okay to eat'. However, she has learned that adopting a lovely self-carriage pose as we walk along will result in a click&treat. In other words, she has learned a new and different way of foraging when she is connected to me with a rope and walking on a paved road.

Some trail riders carry treats and ask trail users they meet to give their horse a treat so that rather than spooking at people with big packs, walking with dogs or riding bicycles, the horse has a reason to look forward to meeting someone on the trail.

The click&treat dynamic is so powerful, and so motivating, that it can be used to 'free-shape' a desired behavior. This means you hang around in a non-agenda but observant way until the horse (or any critter) does something you really like, at which point you click and treat. It works well to teach horses to do all sorts of things. The links below are all in my *Free-shaping* playlist:

- drop the head (*Head Lowering* 1 and 2)
- touch a target (*Clicker 1 with Smoky*)
- pick things up
- follow a bicycle (*Boots and bicycle*)
- bow
- walk along beside the handler
- ring a bell (*Free-shaping Learning to Ring a Bell*)
- tummy tucks

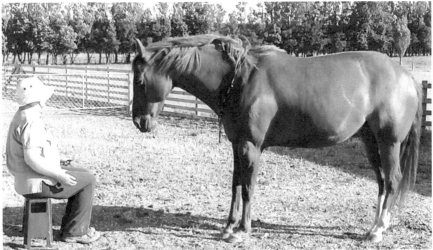

Figure 11: Boots doing her tummy tucks or belly crunches. It's hard to show in a still picture, but she is pushing her weight onto her hindquarters and pulling up her abdominal muscles.

If you can put up your hand or stick to keep your horse out of your personal space, you can teach him not to mug you. Having food on your person does not have to become a problem. Mares carry their milk, but when it comes to natural weaning time, they have no problem telling their youngster that the milk bar is closed.

We teach the horse that a treat is always a consequence of an action that we want. A treat is never something he can demand by being belligerent or pushy. This is an important distinction. It's fine to have your horse be a confident and cheeky pet, but he must always respect your space and the fact that you decide when the treat is given.

We carry out our 'responsibility of care' by being effective and fair. Inconsistency lies at the root of all failures in training. Inconsistency is probably the hardest thing to overcome.

Horses tell us what they think of us by how they treat us. We can't be in charge of how the horse behaves, but we can be totally in charge of how we behave in relation to the horse. How we behave will influence how the horse behaves in our company.

It's apparent that blanket statements about the use of food to motivate or reward are not helpful. Hopefully these notes have given you a wider awareness of how food can be used to help horses enjoy their time with us. If you don't use clicker training but would like to experiment with it, Appendix 1 outlines a way to get started.

Chapter 2

Handler Skills

We need a few skills to get the most out of learning Universal Horse Language. You may already have these skills in abundance. If you are new to horses, you'll develop the skills as you progress through the eight exercises.

The five skills I want to talk about in this book include:
- reading horse body language
- energy management
- handling body extensions (swishies)
- reinforcement
- emotional neutrality.

Reading Horse Body Language

The following notes are taken from my book, *Conversations with Horses: An In-depth look at Signals & Cues Between Horses and their Handlers*. The book has much detail that may be useful if you have limited experience with horses.

A: Signs of a horse in a state of mental, emotional and physical relaxation:

- soft, relaxed tail (will lift tail if we gently rub under it)
- floppy ear tips
- soft eyes
- lowered head (poll level with the withers)
- relaxed, loose or floppy bottom lip

- soft body outline
- relaxed cocked hip
- curiosity with a soft aspect
- if in motion, a soft outline; poll level with withers and rhythmic movement
- happy to stay in our presence
- able to respond to a light signal.

B: Signs of a horse releasing tension:

- sighing
- chewing/licking (not related to food)
- yawning
- shaking head/neck (not related to flies)
- blowing out
- extreme blinking.

C: Signs of Excitement:

Excitement has its own body language:
- head & tail go up
- the whole body becomes bouncy
- the horse strongly needs to move his feet.

It is usually an adrenalin rush based on novelty or enthusiasm rather than fear. A combination of excitement and anxiety can see the tail very high (even straight up with some horses) and the horse becomes unusually large.

D: Signs of a horse expressing annoyance or responding to pain:

- swishing tail (in a continuum from a quick flick to full-fledged tail-wringing)
- ears pinned (which is different from ears just back)
- snaking of neck toward the cause of annoyance (another horse, dog, person)
- turning butt toward the annoyance as a warning that a kick could follow
- if wearing a bit, gaping mouth, constant mouthing trying to adjust the bit's position to be less painful, hanging the tongue out of the side of the mouth
- hesitant or reluctant to move smoothly under saddle
- bucking under saddle
- rearing
- rushing, under saddle, in attempt to get away from the pain/annoyance
- rushing, balking when led in-hand
- moving away from our influence if he is able to.

E: Signs of anxiety or fear-based stress:

- whole body tension
- high head
- staring eyes
- stiff ears
- tight lips
- tightly clamped tail, J-shaped tail if fear is extreme
- desire to move feet away from the situation – always a first response and why most people use ropes and small pens
- the dropped head of a horse that has gone 'internal' – a sort of non-blinking paralysis called catalepsy.

(Chapter 1 looked in more detail at fear responses in horses and in people.)

F: Signs of a horse acting in self-defence:

- leaving our presence is the first choice; but if that is not possible,
- biting
- striking with front leg
- kicking with hind leg
- charging
- rearing if forward movement is blocked.

Ears in Detail

While we are actively engaged with the horse it's not easy to keep an eye on the running commentary of a horse's ears. It's easier to observe ears in a video. Ears are only one part of the horse's body language, but it's useful to increase our 'ear awareness' as much as we can.

Alert — forward, scanning in anxious mode

Curious/Interested — forward with head movement up or down to focus the eyes

Attentive — forward to what is going on

Back/Sideways - Anxious — only the context of the situation and the rest of the horse's body language can tell us if the ears are back due to anxiety (very stiff), or back because the horse is strongly focusing on a task (not as stiff)

Back/Sideways - Floppy — a chilled out, resting or casually moseying along horse often has the ears half back in a relaxed state.

Pinned — truly pinned ears are a very strong signal that all is not well and other action will follow if things don't change immediately. Some horses lay their ears almost flat when they are strongly focusing on a complex task. This can be more like a 'frown' of concentration and we have to be careful not to presume the ears are pinned and take evasive/inhibitory action that will confuse the horse who was just busy thinking his way through a problem.

It pays to give the horse the benefit of any doubt and read the overall situation and body language rather than just the ears. *Truly pinned ears are unmistakable*, once seen. They are usually accompanied by a very angry face overall and are often followed by snaky-neck movement toward the cause of annoyance.

Working Ears: Back or Sideways, Focused/Thinking — some horses put their ears to the back or side when they are in thinking mode.

We often see these sorts of ear positions in horses doing their job of the moment; e.g., cutting horses, calf-roping horses, dressage horses, horses doing an Agility course.

Because they are carrying out a learned pattern in a known environment, their mind is focused on the task at hand and the precise signals coming from their handler. Their ears often resemble the ears of a dog working sheep. Back and full of concentration on the job.

The ears may resemble that of an irritated or disgruntled horse but if the horse is doing his job and his overall tension and body expression suggest that he is focused, we are probably seeing his personal *working expression*.

Often, as soon as the horse has finished a part of his job, the ears pop forward before the next obstacle or cow or whatever.

It's helpful to watch video clips focusing just on the horse's ears. Usually they are constantly in motion and give us an insight into what may be going on in the horse's mind. Obviously, we can never be sure, but we can get a good idea.

Each horse's ear expressions will follow the same general pattern, but at the same time be unique, so we have to be careful about generalizing too much between horses.

Energy Management

Whatever your horse has just done or is doing when you relax, is what he will note as the right thing to do. When a horse is unsure about what you want, he will experiment with all kinds of moves. It's important to respect this experimentation and not make the horse feel wrong. If things get too far off target, we quietly reset the task in a way that allows us to try again.

If we relax the moment we spot (or feel) the best approximation to what we want, the horse will feel the change in our energy and be willing to try that move again.

We gradually build on this first effort, refining it over time until we get exactly what we want. This is the process of recognizing the smallest try and carefully shaping the behavior until we achieve clear two-way communication.

Whenever the horse slips into reactive or worried mode, it's essential that we reset back to where the horse's confidence returns. To make progress, both the horse and the handler have to be in a confident, thinking frame of mind.

If we find ourselves becoming reactive worried, or fearful, it's equally important that we take a step back and reconsider what we are doing. Often, we don't realize how much pressure we are putting on ourselves until we learn to stop, breathe, take the pressure off, and re-group. Stopping to reflect and allowing a fresh start usually brings new understanding.

We affect a horse when we:

- look at him
- approach him

- face him front on
- touch him with our hand or body extension
- make ourselves larger
- breathe in
- raise our body energy
- show up with treats to use for reward reinforcement (clicker training)
- gesture with our hand or body extension
- give unclear signals
- use inconsistent signals
- ask something that is beyond the horse's physical, mental or emotional ability to deliver at that time
- put the horse into an unusual situation
- rush things - go too fast with new learning
- are fearful - horses sense fear pheromones easily
- are sneaky - predators are sneaky so horses are highly attuned to sneakiness
- lose our cool - the horse can only be as calm and cool as we are
- correct too much, which makes the horse unwilling to try again
- change routines suddenly.

We enable our horse to relax when we:

- look away
- turn away
- move away
- shrink our size
- relax our body energy
- take up neutral body language and body extension positions
- use clear, consistent signals
- stay emotionally neutral or even better, are laughing having fun - horses easily pick up happy vibrations

- spend dwell time together to pause during a teaching/learning session
- spend 'down time' together where all we do is hang out
- use reward reinforcement (clicker training) correctly
- recognize thresholds and retreat to where both we and the horse can find relaxation
- recognize when we need to deal with our own thresholds first
- pause and set up a task again, rather than correct a mistake
- honor the routines we've set up
- rubbing and massage – some horses enjoy this but others don't and will see it as more pressure.

As we become more aware of what we are doing and how we are doing it, we gradually learn to adjust our behavior more quickly, so giving the horse the best deal possible.

Signals

I prefer the word 'signal' rather than 'cue' because, by definition, a signal means the same thing to the sender and the receiver. If we go through the process of carefully teaching the horse the meaning of a signal, we have achieved clear two-way communication.

Signals often arise naturally out of the teaching process. If we want to teach a horse to back up, a touch on the chest generally makes sense. We can add a simultaneous voice signal and soon the horse will respond willingly to touch or voice.

During the teaching and learning stage, we may have to exaggerate our signal until the horse is clear about what we mean. It also helps to use objects and obstacles as props to limit the horse's choices and make it easier for him to do what we want. Once the understanding is reached, we gradually remove the props. Our signals can turn into requests invisible except to a knowledgeable observer.

I've devoted a whole book to the topic of signals. It's called *Conversations with Horses: An In-depth Look at Signals and Cues between Horses and their Handlers*. Here is a summary of a few key points about signals.

On-off signals, for example asking for a transition. We turn on a signal to ask the horse to trot, then turn if off again. The flow of our energy with the trotting gait gives the horse on-going information about staying in the gait. When we want to slow from a trot to a walk, we use one or more specific signals for the transition such as a weight shift, a voice signal or lifting the rein hand. We turn off the signal for the downward transition as soon as the horse complies.

Constant on signals, for example asking for the horse to move sideways. We keep the signal on until we want the movement to stop.

Primary signals arise naturally from what you want the horse to do. For example, to ask the horse to step back, we put signal pressure with our hand on the nose or on the halter. We release the pressure as soon as the horse steps back.

Secondary signals: If we always say, "Back," when we use the primary touch signal, the voice, "Back," signal becomes a secondary signal and can work as effectively as the primary one.

Touch signals are a main part of riding and daily husbandry such as haltering, leading, grooming and foot care.

Gesture signals can be used to direct the horse's bubble when we are playing on the ground.

Unconscious signals are ones we give without realizing it. These include our emotional state. Horses can read our emotional state in a heartbeat and it is a strong signal for them. That's why learning about and achieving emotional neutrality is so important. If we can breathe easily, chuckle, laugh and generally be relaxed, the horse will buy into our mood. If we are uptight, the horse has little chance to be at ease. He will mirror our body tension.

Presence signal: Our arrival in the horse's environment is a signal in itself. If we are relaxed and not paying the horse any attention, we are sending a certain sort of signal. We may be there to clean the paddock or pull weeds. If we approach the horse intending to interact with him, we are sending a signal. Many horses know instantly whether their person is carrying a halter or not. Horses respond continuously to all environmental cues and we are obviously part of their environment.

Environmental signals: A horse trailer is an example of an environmental signal. A trailer might suggest a resting spot and a trip home to one horse. It could elicit a huge "No!" response from another horse. Environmental signals can be deeply lodged in a horse's brain, e.g., a horse may refuse to step into soft ground due to a past traumatic experience of getting stuck in deep mud.

Environmental signals are constantly changing with weather, light, wind, seasons, critters. Environmental signals are also the spaces, objects and obstacles we use for training and gymnastic exercises. If we consistently ask for a transition in the same spot, the horse will relate the transition to the spot.

An awareness of the types of signals we use, and how they influence our relationship with a horse, allows us to see the truth in the old horseman's saying, "Nothing means nothing to a horse." Or conversely, 'everything means something to a horse'. Horses are many times more astute and observant than people.

Handling Body Extensions: The Swishies

'Swishies' is the term I use for a flexible body extension. It allows us to be more horse-like by making our body longer or taller as needed. Horses find it difficult to read the intent of our tall bodies as compared to the long body of another horse. The swishies also allow us to enlarge our personal bubble to keep ourselves safe if a horse's behavior becomes intrusive.

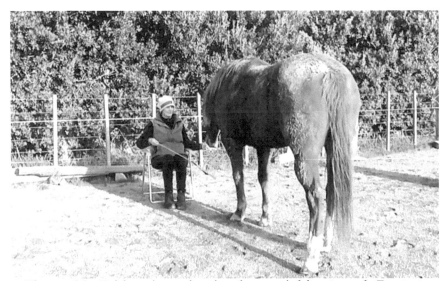

Figure 12: Bridget is activating her swishies to ask Boots to stand back a bit while they are Sharing Time and Space. Sometimes Boots' nibbling can change from gentle curiosity to intimidating.

If we carry the swishies as a matter of course, the horse sees them as part of our body. Horse usually keep their neck, tail and legs in neutral, but if they want to send a message, they activate their neck, tail and legs to make their message clear. In the same way, we carry our swishies in neutral and only activate them to clarify our intent for the horse. They are never used in an aggressive, punishing manner.

Swishies are different from fiberglass sticks in that they can be swished to disturb the air near the horse. Horses are very sensitive to this and will avoid the disturbed air. This means we can enlarge our personal space without needing to touch the horse.

I always use them by swishing toward the horse's feet and moving up to the height of his knees if necessary.

A similar air-swirly effect can be achieved with a rope or a six-foot piece of cord twirled like a helicopter blade. This is good to know if we unexpectedly come across a pushy horse and need to enlarge our personal space. It allows us to be safe without any aggressive actions toward the horse. Horses understand the concept of personal space. They also know the difference between assertion of our own space and aggression toward their space.

I have an old carriage whip that gives a good swishing effect. A bit of white cloth taped to the end makes it easier for the horse to see. A couple of long dressage whips are also effective.

Alternatively, something like long springy willow twigs give a better swishing effect than commercial whips. The idea is to use what you have available and keep alert for something that you might like better.

As already mentioned, the purpose of the swishies is to function as an extension of our body. Also, as mentioned earlier, horses have a hard time understanding the shape of our tall, upright bodies. We can use the swishies to emulate another horse's neck, tail or leg. The swishies allow us to make our personal bubble bigger and they allow us to disturb the air around our horse's bubble when we need him to move.

The purpose of our body extensions is not to assault the horse in any way, but to accentuate our body language in a way that resembles the actions of another horse.

Reinforcement

Whether we are horse or human, our future actions are based on the consequences of actions we've taken in the past. If something we did resulted in a consequence that we liked, we will tend to do it again. If an action resulted in a consequence we didn't like, we will tend to not do it again, or do less of it.

Most of us engage in paid work because the money we earn allows us to buy the necessities of life such as food and shelter. We may not love our job, but the positive consequence of the paycheck keeps us showing up and doing the work.

When we are teaching our horse, there are two ways we can give him a consequence that he values.

1. We can apply pressure and remove the pressure when the horse responds in the way we want. This is how most trainers operate. Horses value the comfort of the release.
2. We can wait around until the horse does something we like, and give him a high-value food treat the moment he does it. This is called free-shaping. It is a technique often used by clicker trainers. Unless afraid or upset, horses value a tasty morsel.

Clicker training uses a marker signal (click or special sound) at the very moment the horse is doing what we want. The marker signal is promptly followed by a small food treat that the horse likes.

Since waiting around until the horse does something we want to train would be restricted to things that horses do naturally, there is a distinct limit to using only free-shaping.

Clicker trainers use the best of both reinforcement systems. They apply signal pressure and when the horse responds in the desired way, they release the signal pressure and simultaneously click and promptly follow the click with the food reward.

It's easiest to think of these two ways of reinforcing the behaviors we want by calling them:
- release reinforcement (removing pressure)
- reward reinforcement (marking the behavior wanted and adding a treat).

Release and reward reinforcement work nicely hand-in-hand with each other. Horses love the idea of being able to earn instant rewards.

If we use only release reinforcement, horses are limited to experimentation to find what will release the trainer's pressure. When we add reward reinforcement, they pay close attention to discover what will bring forth the click&treat. Indeed, they become proactive about offering the requested behavior at the smallest of signals.

If you don't already use clicker training but would like to explore its potential, Appendix 1 outlines how to get started.

Clicker trained horses are often keen to start their learning sessions and seldom want them to end.

The whole topic of reinforcement is looked at more fully in my book, *How to Create Good Horse Training Plans: The Art of Thin-Slicing*.

Emotional Neutrality

It's easy to get caught up with the emotion our horse expresses if he is in a state of excitement, anxiety or fear. Horses are usually fine until we go to get them and start doing things with them. Most of what people do with horses is totally unrelated to a horse's lifestyle in the wild.

A horse's behavior at any one moment is conditional on the situation in which he finds himself. His behavior can change very quickly as his perception of what is happening changes. Horses are superbly sensitive to changes in people, physical environment and other horses. As with people, some horses are self-confident learners and some horses are by nature much more fearful about every change.

The state of our horse emotionally, physically and mentally right now determines what we need to do next. It may be best to back off or to persist calmly in the correct position until the horse at least tries to follow our request.

When to do what, and for how long, can only be gained by study and experience. We can study to gain the intellectual knowledge needed to help our horse become more comfortable as a domestic animal. Thoughtful practice gives us the experience that puts knowledge into deep muscle memory so it becomes intuitive.

It pays to keep a sense of humor as we go about all this studying and learning. We have to accept that a horse will always be a horse. The better we understand what it must be like to be a horse, the easier it will be to keep our emotions neutral when we face training challenges. When things don't go well, emotional neutrality allows us to 'put the horse home' and walk away to consider options for the way forward.

Being prey animals, horses are wired to be constantly aware of changes that might mean danger. Flight (move those feet) is their default response if they get worried. We must acknowledge this, accept it and respect it.

One member of a horse-human partnership has to be cool and calm at all times. Since we removed the horse from his natural environment to be with us, we probably have to try hard to be the cool and calm member.

To be a good trainer and companion for a horse, learning to communicate with language that the horse understands is a big step in a good direction. Learning and using Universal Horse Language sets a foundation of mutual understanding on which we can base further training. It's our responsibility to teach the horse the life skills he needs to live in a human-dominated world.

When horses are confident and understand what we want, they will usually do it gracefully. They have no desire to be wrong or bad. In reactive mode, the horse is, at all times, doing what he thinks he has to do in that moment to stay safe. We have to know what to do to keep ourselves and others safe if the horse slips into reactive mode.

If a confident, imaginative horse is in thinking mode and not kept busy enough with interesting challenges, he may initiate games to keep himself amused. These may be designed to see who he can push around, as horses do with each other to sort out their social order.

The senior partner in a relationship is the one with the plan and the focus on the plan. If your plan falters, a horse in thinking mode will fill the gap with his own ideas. A worried or reactive horse will sense your lack of confidence and get more anxious.

Nothing our horse does is ever a personal affront to us. He's just being a horse. He is trying to keep himself safe, amused, or he is testing boundaries.

It is up to us to build our horse's confidence in many situations; to give the thinking horse enough fun and variety, and the reactive horse enough consistency until he knows for sure what we want.

Emotion neutrality is a skill that helps us be the companion and teacher that a horse deserves. At the first feeling of anger, fear, frustration or nervousness, we can learn to:
- back off
- breathe deeply
- walk away
- calm down
- think about what just happened
- gather more information
- change our plan
- improve our gear handling skills

We can learn how to create plans to move forward in the direction we want. There is lots of detail about this in my book, *How to Create Good Horse Training Plans: The Art of Thin-Slicing.*

We can stop a session any time. We can always start again later. If we push through with our negative emotions, we will harm and undermine our relationship with the horse. Punishment doesn't work with horses because, being prey animals, they see aggressive behavior as a predator attempting to kill and eat them. It's important that we can accept their reality as being very different from our human reality.

Learning is a messy process. This is true for humans and horses. Don't expect the process to look like the final product. Be happy with 2% improvement each session. Celebrate each small success. Set realistic goals. Realistic goals are ones that you know both you and your horse can achieve successfully in the next little while. Be prepared to give learning a new task as long as it takes, without the date of an outside event affecting what you do.

How Long will it Take?

An example that Boots and I are working on right now is to walk along with Boots holding a riding crop in her mouth. It was one of ten tricks in a fun Horse Agility course. Boots has never worn a bit for riding or driving, so carrying something in her mouth other than food is a new concept for her.

I'm aware that having something in the mouth activates salivation which in turn activates stomach juices. This is a likely reason why many horses ridden in a bit develop stomach ulcers. But since I am going to click&treat after a few steps of carrying something, food is part of the process, so I decided to teach it as a new challenge for both of us.

In our Horse Agility Tricks competition, she carried a willow twig for ten steps while in the process of eating it. It got through as technically correct, but I don't think it was what the person setting the task had in mind.

Figure 13: Boots and I walking along with Boots carrying something in her mouth. She was eating the willow twig but it did count as one of our ten tricks for a fun Horse Agility class.

We embarked on a training plan to teach her to carry a stick. Our daily morning walks on the road made a perfect venue, because if she dropped the stick (an old riding crop with the outer colored plastic coating removed) it didn't get covered in sand.

We've been playing with it several times a week for about six weeks. At the time of writing, we often get ten to fifteen steps before we halt, I put my hand on the stick and she earns a click&treat. Often, I settle for less so that I can click&treat before she drops it. When she does drop it, I say, "Oh no," in a sad voice, pick it up and we walk on.

Boots has a strong habit of taking up a fancy self-carriage with lovely poll flexion. We've created this with reward reinforcement during our walks over the years. Instead of earning click&treat for twenty steps of self-carriage, I offer her the stick when she offers the self-carriage. It's a way she can tell me that she's ready to try again.

Over time we'll get more consistency. It is a work in progress and illustrates how lots of very small attempts can gradually build a new habit or skill.

How slowly or quickly a particular horse is able to absorb and become confident with new learning varies a great deal.

The mindmap that follows is taken from Chapter 6 of my book, *How to Create Good Horse Training Plans*.

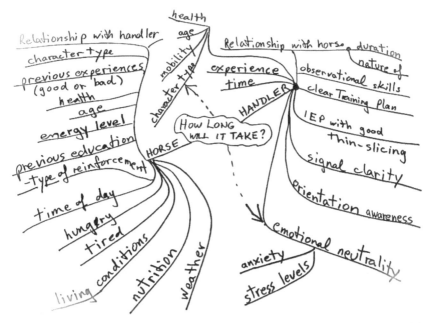

Figure 14: It's hard to say how long it takes to teach something because there are so many variables.

Emotional neutrality relates to the energy we carry as an aura that horses recognize in an instant. A horse can pick up our pleasure and joy when he does something well. He equally picks up every hint of frustration or annoyance. By the time we recognize that we are annoyed or angry, the horse will have withdrawn from the closeness of the relationship.

It takes a long time to build the trust of a prey animal wired for flight. A moment of aggression can erase a great deal of trust. We must never forget that the first instinct of prey animals is to leave when they feel pressure.

As mentioned earlier, we have to accept that nothing a horse does is ever a personal affront to us. What a horse does, in any one moment, is what he feels he needs to do because he is a horse. He may feel he needs to:

- stay safe (move his feet to escape, or withdraw into his secret self)
- eat

- amuse himself
- check out an opportunity to rise in the social order (challenge our seniority)
- seek companionship and cling to it.

Confident, imaginative type horses tend to seek opportunities to rise in the social order and seem to enjoy testing their humans often to see if they are still worthy. It is important to not see this as naughtiness, but as a strong-willed horse being his natural self.

We have taken the horse away from his natural herd situation and put ourselves in place of his horse companions. If he accepts us as a member of his group, he will behave toward us as he would to another group member. That is why it is important to maintain our position as higher in the social order firmly but fairly. The exercises of Universal Horse Language gradually lead us into this position and keep us there. Conscious development of emotional neutrality allows us to respond to the horse as his senior partner, rather than become reactive ourselves.

As we become more aware of what our body language is probably saying to the horse, it becomes easier to reduce the anxiety, frustration and fear that might lead to aggression or withdrawal on our part. As we gain skills of communication and teach our horse (in a systematic way) what we require him to do, our emotional neutrality will get stronger and stronger.

We all like a companion who is clear, confident and fair. Horses are the same. Because horses are super-sensitive to body language and energy auras, they read our mood in a split second.

People really good with horses have emotional neutrality because they know from experience that what they are doing will lead to the result they want, even though the process may look nothing like the final product. The rest of us get a horse and try to head directly for some final product we imagine in our mind.

People really good with horses have become good because they are naturally observant and empathetic. They devote

study and time to gain the knowledge and experience needed to make being with horses like second nature. They know:
- how horses communicate with each other
- when to add pressure to clarify a signal
- when to remove pressure and relax
- when to wait
- when to quit a session.

Skills Summary

Set realistic goals for yourself and the horse. You know a goal is realistic when you can break it down into a series of very small steps (slices), the first of which you feel confident about doing right now.

Have a plan. Keep it flexible so you can suit it to your horse as he is in the moment. Make sure the horse's learning needs stay in charge of the pace of learning, not a date on a calendar or someone else's urging. It is easy to lose your own confidence if another person attempts to push you too far out of your comfort zones too fast, either your horse's comfort zone or your own.

Organize your environment to help make the moves you want easy for the horse, and the moves you don't want more difficult. Ideally work in an area where the horse can see his companions but they are not able to interfere.

Think ahead about risk factors and manage them. Make no assumptions.

Record your goals and record what you did and how it went.

Strive to not make the horse feel wrong while he is learning or if he loses his confidence. Learners don't make mistakes. They are in the process of learning, which is experimenting with what not to do, as well as what to do. Same goes for you.

Always give the horse the benefit of the doubt. Often they are responding to signals we are not even aware we are giving. It never hurts to stop and start again. Clarity of communication is our constant goal. If we are unclear, horses will try to fill in with what they thought we meant. But a horse could also be testing your knowledge, resolve and persistence. The better you can learn to read the horse, the easier it will be to make the right judgement about what is going on. See what is happening from the horse's point of view. Put yourself into his life.

We make progress by taking what the horse is able to offer already and shape that into what we want as the finished tools. Learn to recognize where the horse is emotionally, mentally and physically in the moment at hand. Then you can decide how you can best ask him to follow your next suggestion.

Begin a teaching phase within your session only when the horse is in thinking mode. If he becomes unconfident or reactive, go back to something you can both do easily, wait, think, regroup, start again later or next session. Wait for signs of relaxation such as exhaling, blowing out, rapid blinking, lowering head, chewing. It's quite illuminating to try these yourself if you notice you are getting tense.

Encourage the horse's curiosity at every opportunity. Get him to follow new things, rather than approach him with them.

Be consistent with your signals but not boring with your activities. End each session on a good note. If you are running out of time, do something you can both do confidently and stop there. Frequent short sessions of three to five minutes' work well for teaching many things.

Avoid drilling. After two or three good tries or having achieved your mini-goal, do something else and come back to it again later or next session.

Keep 'new stuff' teaching sessions short but long enough to note a positive change (can be a tiny change) in the horse. Intersperse them with improving the quality of activities already learned, or you could just relax and hang out together.

Learn to recognize when your horse is reaching his limit in a teaching session and try to reach this limit but not go over it. This will come with experience. During one session, a useful balance to aim for is about 80% warm-up, relaxed groundwork or riding, cool-down and 20% concentrated focused maneuvers or new learning. Recognize your own limits too. Be happy with 2% improvement over last time. Recognize and celebrate and record tiny improvements, both in your horse and in yourself.

Build in 'wait time' or 'dwell time'. This is time during your sessions when you remove all pressure to give the horse time to digest what is going on.

Stay with a new learning task for at least seven to nine sessions, then every second session for seven to nine times, then occasionally to keep it refreshed. Some things with some horses will take much longer. Usually one day equals one session. With clicker training, one session is very short and it really helps if you can do three or four small (5-minute) sessions in a day, tucked in among other things you are doing that day. See Appendix 1 for information about clicker training.

Interrupt negative behavior patterns by directing the horse's energy into a task you know he can do; e.g., lower head, back up, step sideways, put nose on something.

Expect to have to re-teach lessons:
- in new environments
- asking at liberty, or if you trained at liberty, asking with rope attached
- asking for more energy (e.g. trot instead of walk, canter instead of trot)
- whenever your horse shows he has lost confidence.

Chapter 3 begins our look at the eight exercises that teach us Universal Horse Language.

Chapter 3

Communicating Zero Intent

'Zero Intent' is being in our horse's presence without asking him to do anything. As long as he remains polite and we feel safe, we just want to hang out with the horse in the same way that horses hang out with each other.

Exercise 1: Quiet Sharing of Time and Space

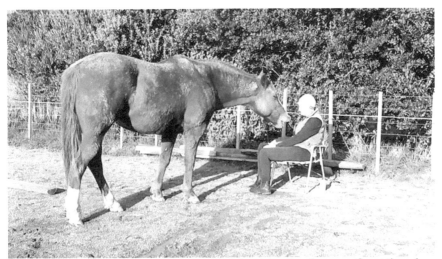

Figure 15: Boots is smiling at Bridget in the hope of getting her to dispense a treat.

You need, for your one-on-one dates with your horse:
- a largish, safe enclosed area
- as few distractions as possible (another horse nearby, but separate, can be helpful to keep a worried horse at ease when you first begin *Quiet Sharing of Time and Space*)

- a chair
- reading material (your glasses?)
- two swishies
- carrots stashed under your chair for a shy horse, or in two or three locations just outside your fence (plastic screw top containers work well), for a friendly horse
- your horse at liberty
- time to relax into the horse sense of being 'in the moment'.

Learning something new and meaningful always requires a lot of mental, physical and emotional energy, especially when first getting started. *Quiet Sharing of Time and Space* becomes something you can do with your horse forever, whenever you have time.

To help with the nuts and bolts of starting this exercise, I've created three checklists. Once a person has the nuts and bolts of all eight exercises sorted, creativity can creep in. The skills developed with the exercises can be used organically as they seem to best fit any situation.

Read all three checklists before you get started.

Checklist 1: INTELLECTUAL – Getting Your Head Ready

Figure 16: It's up to you to decide how much close contact you are comfortable with.

In Figure 16, Bridget is comfortable with receiving a kiss from Boots. As long as you don't feel intimidated, it's fine to let a polite horse get up close and personal. Be aware if nudging might turn into nipping.

#75 HorseGym with Boots demonstrates the process. There are also 3 older but quite interesting clips in my *Universal Horse Language* playlist.

1. The purpose of *Quiet Sharing of Time and Space* is to get you accepted as part of your horse's in-group. Horses can perceive us either as something to be eternally wary of, or as part of their personal group.
2. Wary horses will remain poised on the edge of fear and flight. They feel unsafe around people and they will *be unsafe* around people.
3. Horses that see you as part of their in-group will relate to you as they relate to other horses as long as you consistently use Universal Horse Language and remain within the boundaries of their understanding.

4. The purpose of all training or educating of domestic horses is obviously to enlarge their boundaries of understanding, so making them bolder and more reliable in various situations.
5. *Quiet Sharing of Time and Space* allows you to become more like a horse. It puts you in the zone where time by the clock doesn't exist, where life follows the natural rhythms of day and night, of seasons, of looking for food, of being constantly aware of danger, of interacting with group members. This can be a big stretch for some people. Other people find it hugely relaxing and life-enhancing.

Figure 17: Bridget is enjoying the sun while Boots grazes. How long we relax with our horse depends on what we can fit into our lifestyle. Frequent short dates with our horse are just as effective as longer dates.

6. *Quiet Sharing of Time and Space* allows time for the horse to accept your relaxed presence in his space. This can be a huge stretch for some horses who have only had demanding and/or predator-like interactions with people. Other horses may be all over you like a rash and need to be shown how to stand back politely.

7. Be mentally prepared to move your chair if the horse gets too overbearing. There is a fine line between friendly exploration with nose and lips, and seeing if you can be pushed around. Moving your chair tells your overbearing horse that you don't want to be near him right now. It is what horses do. They just move away. In this situation moving away is a neutral action. If he follows you and continues to be overbearing, you'll use your body language and swishies to ask him to back out of your space (as described in numbers 12 – 15).
8. When you move your chair, position it *side-on* to the horse, not facing him.
9. Sit outside the enclosure fence if you feel unsafe inside it.
10. Realize you will need to *experiment* with understanding when your horse is investigating you, when he is pushing on you, when you should move your chair or ask him to back off.
11. It's by experimenting that you start to get the feeling for the whole exercise. No one can give you a recipe. Every partnership is different. You'll begin to *feel* what is probably the right thing to do next.
12. Understand the powerful effect of the swishies to expand your bubble and make the horse back off or move away any time you feel intimidated.
13. Pushing the horse away too strongly at first is better than not being strong enough. If you are not strong enough, you are teaching the horse that he doesn't have to pay attention. Your signals turn into nagging. If you are too strong at first, you can always get lighter next time.
14. If the horse is being overbearing, push him away strongly enough and far enough so he doesn't want to come back right away. In other words, avoid nagging him back repeatedly. Be sure in your mind and be

clear to him, that you don't want him around for a while. Make being near you a bit of a privilege.
15. Use assertive (not aggressive) body language. Horses higher in the group's social order use their energy to enlarge their personal space as necessary to re-direct the behavior of others.

Checklist Two: PHYSICAL – Keeping You Both Safe and Comfortable

1. You need a safe, secure place to hang out together, e.g. a roomy corral or a small paddock. You can separate a corner of an arena or a big paddock or a nice shady area under a tree by using electric fence tape (not electrified).
2. Allocate time daily as frequently as possible.
3. Sort out two swishies — supple willow twigs, bamboo canes or dressage whips about 130cm long. These allow you to enlarge your personal bubble for your own safety. They allow you to disturb the air at the edge of the horse's bubble if you want to move him away. There is usually no need to touch the horse with the swishies.

Figure 18: Bridget is using her swishies to ask Boots to step back after she got a bit overbearing and intimidating.

4. Get another person to use the swishies on your bubble. Ask them to start swishing at ground level right and left (not up and down), then move up (still swishing right to left) until they are swishing above your head. Note your physical and emotional reactions.
5. Use the swishies on other people and get both their physical, emotional and verbal responses.
6. Always begin with assertive body language before you activate the swishies.
7. Use as much assertive body and swishy energy as you need to move a pushy horse, but, once he understands, don't use more than you need to make your point that he has to move.
8. Have carrot strips (or treats of your choice) to *reward* polite behavior. For a timid horse, keep the treats under your chair to act as a draw card for him to come and see you. For a pushy horse, keep them outside the enclosure in screw top plastic containers, but you can also have them under your chair if you want the horse to push on you so you can teach him to be polite by rewarding him when he stands back and relaxes. If you use clicker training all the time, your normal treat pouch may be fine.
9. Comfortable chair.
10. Absorbing book, magazine or smartphone (glasses).
11. Grazing or hay for the horse is optional at this point. Ideally you want your horse feeling well fed before your date. To learn the procedure, it's easier to be in a grassless or well-grazed area.
12. With little or nothing to eat in your 'dating' enclosure, he will pay more attention to you, which is what you want at the beginning. It makes it easier to read his intentions and relate to him. Being in a non-grazing area allows you to either entice him with carrots (shy horse), or teach him to stand back politely to receive a treat (pushy horse).

13. For some sessions, you could put out several piles of hay. This will allow you to seamlessly move into the *Claiming the Spot* exercise when you feel ready. If you don't want hay on an arena surface you could use big tubs, carpets, tarps, sheets or blankets.
14. Eventually, once the horse is confident and polite, it's nice to do *Quiet Sharing of Time and Space* in the horse's usual grazing environment.

Checklist Three: EMOTIONAL – Getting Your Heart Ready

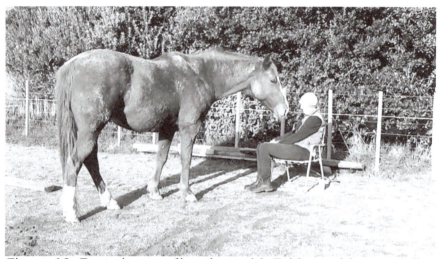

Figure 19: Boots is spending time with Bridget without needing to push on her. They can relax in each other's company and enjoy the sunny winter afternoon together.

1. Let go of expectations, goals, presumptions, anxiety.
2. Just start, and know it will improve each time you get out there.
3. Nothing will be perfect; learning is a messy business.
4. No one cares except you and your horse (and other people studying this).

5. Others may laugh at you and think you are peculiar. That's their privilege.
6. Others may be really interested. It's up to you how much (or little) you want to tell them.
7. Observe your horse without staring directly at him.
8. Observe (without making value judgements) what your horse is actually doing.
9. For a session or two, you could wear a watch and record exactly what your horse is doing at regular time intervals (e.g., every two minutes or every five minutes). If this interests you, it is a great study in itself, especially if you can also do it when the horse is in a paddock interacting with other horses. You may begin to see interesting patterns.
10. Appreciate that everything the horse does is FEEDBACK. Feedback can be positive, negative or neutral and all of it has the same value.
11. For this exercise of becoming more horse-like, you need to let go of all your horsemanship aims, goals, desires and dreams. I doubt that horses dream positively of people on their backs, driving them forward over, through and into things for no reason the horse can see (other than to get it over with).
12. You can retrieve your goals when you need them and play with making your goals your horse's goals. But first you need to understand his goals by observing and listening to his body language.
13. Be prepared to move your chair if the horse gets overbearing. This is a neutral action.

Figure 20: Bridget is moving her chair because Boots became a bit too overwhelming. Moving our chair away from the horse resembles another horse walking away to gain more personal space. It is an alternative to asking the horse to step back using the swishies.

14. When you sit down, put your chair side-on to the horse. Try to not stare directly at him.
15. Be ready to defend your bubble with your assertive (not aggressive) body language and your swishies as necessary to stay safe. Being with a horse requires our *risk management radar* to be on at all times.
16. Be ready to notice when your pushy horse is standing back politely. Casually stand up, get a treat from where you stashed them and walk over to him to give it to him, then go sit down again. He might follow you right back to your chair and give you another opportunity to ask him to stand back politely.
17. At first expect only a few seconds of politeness, then gradually ask him to wait longer and longer before you get the treat. Watch for signs that he is relaxing while standing away from you (sighing, licking, chewing, head shaking, head lowering, cocked hind leg, relaxed tail, relaxed ears, soft eyes).

The Shy, Anxious, Flighty, Timid or Suspicious Horse
1. Notice when your shy horse is getting bolder. Before you start, put out a feed dish he is familiar with, well away from your chair.
2. When you notice him glancing at you, walk to his dish and drop in a treat. Then go sit down again.
3. As the horse becomes more confident, you can put the feed dish closer and closer to your chair. Look for the signs of relaxation (sighing, licking, chewing, head shaking, head lowering, cocked hind leg, relaxed tail, relaxed ears, soft eyes).
4. Success for both of you is when he will come and accept treats out of the dish in your lap, or out of your hand. It could happen in a day or two or it could take weeks.

Chapter 4 looks at how to begin communication once the horse is totally comfortable with our quiet presence sitting in his enclosure.

Chapter 4

Zero Intent While the Handler is in Motion

The next two exercises build on the horse's acceptance of having us sit and relax in a shared space. We'll start to move around the horse's enclosure, but we'll have no intention for him to do anything other than occasionally greet us by putting his nose on our hand, if he wants to.

> **Exercise 2: Active Sharing of Time and Space**. The horse stays relaxed while a) you move quietly around the enclosure and b) you also gently move the swishies as you walk around calmly with no intent. We call this: *Active Sharing of Time and Space.*
>
> **Exercise 3: Greet & Go**. You approach the horse from the front, stretch your arm out, palm down (with a relaxed hand) and allow the horse to make the final contact. As soon as he does, you quietly move away.

The Swishies in Neutral

It's important that the horse recognizes when the swishies don't mean anything. You don't want the horse to see you as a constant ON signal when you are walking around his home.

The swishies become like another horse's tail. The tail is in neutral unless the horse wants to send a message. A horse swishing his tail actively (other than swishing flies) sends an easily understood message.

In the same way, our swishies can be in neutral. They can be still, or moving gently like a tail swishing flies. If the need arises, our swishies can, like a horse's tail, swish forcefully, i.e. come out of neutral and send a strong message.

Exercise 2: Active Sharing of Time and Space

The purpose of this exercise is to build the horse's confidence with having us moving around his home environment without him feeling that we want him to do something. We move around in the same way as a horse in the same paddock would move around minding his own business.

This procedure is demonstrated in #76 *HorseGym with Boots*.

You want the horse to stay relaxed (hopefully eating hay or grazing) when you move casually around the area with mildly active swishies. You are not focusing on the horse as you move. The horse will come to understand that you are still minding your own business, just like when you were sitting down reading your book. He needs to feel that it is safe for him to mind his own business while you are casually walking around outside his personal bubble with your swishies.

You don't want your mere presence or the fact that you have moved out of your chair to be an instant ON signal to your horse. You want him to be able to relax while you are casually moving around. He'll soon realize that even though you are moving around, you are not asking him to do anything.

Active Sharing of Time and Space is a developmental exercise. Once the horse is relaxed when we wander around his enclosure, it's not something we have to do every day, although cleaning the paddock and pulling weeds create a similar situation.

You need: all the facilities you use for the original *Quiet Sharing of Time and Space* but now you also need several piles of hay in your enclosure, or have the horse in a grazing area. This gives the horse something to do - the option of eating rather than focused on you moving around with your swishies.

Figure 21: Boots is happy to graze while Bridget walks around the paddock gently moving her swishies right and left. We've done this before, so Boots' personal bubble in this situation is quite small. When first introducing this exercise, you'd start much further away from the horse as you experiment to find where the edge of his personal bubble is at that moment.

1. Once you and your horse are comfortable with *Quiet Sharing of Time and Space, i.e.* while you are sitting relaxed in your chair, it's time to get the horse comfortable with you walking around in a casual manner with your swishies.
2. First hold the swishies behind you as if they are your tail. Do that until the horse is ho-hum about you moving around.
3. Start walking a circuit as far away as the enclosure allows. Gradually let your circuit drift closer to the horse. The instant you notice that he is getting concerned (raises his head, stops eating, moves), <u>immediately</u> move further away from him. If you stay true to this part of the exercise, the horse will gradually become less sensitive to your active presence.

4. When wandering about with the swishies behind you is ho-hum for the horse, progress to slowly swishing them right and left in front of you (one in each hand) with the ends at ground level, like someone using a metal detector in each hand.
5. Your intention is not to approach the horse, but to stay well clear of his bubble and wander around fairly aimlessly, swishing. Start with gentle swishing. Stay relaxed and casual.
6. Some horses have a small personal bubble and will be quite unconcerned. They may already be used to friendly handling with stick-like objects such as dressage whips, a Parelli style Carrot Stick™ or a stick&string combination.

The Shy, Anxious, Flighty, Timid or Suspicious Horse

1. Another horse's bubble may be huge. In the first exercise, you probably had to entice him to your chair with treats. Your action of walking around may bring up his adrenalin when you begin this exercise. You know this because he moves away as soon as you become active. He may have had past traumatic experiences with sticks and/or ropes, so his fear and flight may be a conditioned response.
2. With an anxious, flighty type of horse, it's important that your enclosed area is large enough and safe enough for him to move away until he feels able to stop, turn, face you and make decisions.
3. If the horse shows anxiety, *move yourself away* from the horse, never toward him. At the same time, it's very important not to stop doing what you are doing (walking around casually) UNTIL the horse gears down his agitated behavior - even just a little bit.

4. When you see him change down a gear, stop, relax, pause and eventually start moving around again. Sooner or later the horse will notice that you stop when he stops or (at the beginning) when he at least slows down.
5. He'll eventually realize that there's no point in rushing around. Some authors call this whole process desensitization. It could take five minutes or five weeks of daily practice, depending on your horse's background and his innate characteristics. It will also depend on the accuracy of the timing of your correct responses to his behavior - as outlined in numbers 3 and 4 above.
6. When the horse becomes more confident, you can practice varying the intensity of your swishing. Always move <u>away</u> and swish <u>less</u> if the horse shows anxiety.

The Intimidating Horse

A horse may become intimidating because he has learned in the past that a good defence is a strong offense. Usually he is acting from a base of fear and insecurity. Once he understands that you will use the Universal Horse Language exercises clearly and consistently, he will usually become more secure in your relationship.

1. If the horse becomes intimidating, we enlarge our personal bubble by using our swishies as vigorously as required. If the need arises to move the horse away from us, we must use as much energy as it takes to have the horse yield to our request.
2. If we lose our nerve and back away from a horse pushing on us, we have taught him that pushing on us will result in us backing away. This is everyday horse body language. You've just taught the horse that

he can move you. Safety suggests it should be the other way around.

3. Like anything to do with horses, we must have our risk radar on and set up situations that keep everyone safe. If the horse has a history of intimidating people, these are skills he has learned. As mentioned earlier, in his mind a good offense is the best defense. With such a horse, lots of sitting with him on the other side of a fence is helpful to gain his basic acceptance of your presence. At some point, you'll be ready sit on the same side of the fence, but have a quick retreat plan just in case you need it.

4. With such a complex horse, you could begin *Active Sharing of Time and Space* by moving along a fence line remaining on the other side from the horse. It may work to set up electric fencing (not electrified) to partition the space. Or run a temporary fence inside the main fence giving you a track that enables you to walk right around the horse.

5. There will probably be moments when you must focus on the horse with strong intent and ask him to move out of your space. You perhaps did that already if the horse became intimidating while you were sitting in your chair during *Quiet Sharing of Time and Space*.

6. As long as you consistently use as much energy as you need to have the horse move away (but not more than you need) and stay back from you for a while, the horse will learn to back off at your request without question. Your energy drops as soon as the horse gives way to you. You don't carry on and chase the horse once he has backed away from you.

As you play your way through these exercises, the horse will differentiate when you are addressing him and when you are not. Among people, when we are near another person, they understand when we are addressing them and when we are not. We are either looking at them and talking with them or we are minding your own business or talking to someone else. (Think medical waiting rooms, shopping or public transport.) Horses have the same understanding.

Once the horse is unconcerned about you walking around the enclosure, you add in the third exercise which is the *Greet & Go* routine. Every now and then, in-between casual walking around or reading in your chair, approach the horse from the front in a friendly manner and hold out your hand for a nose-to-hand greeting. *Greet & Go* adds a more interactive dimension to *Active Sharing of Time and Space*.

Exercise 3: Greet & Go = Acknowledging Other Group Members

Background

When a new horse is added to an established herd he will (if he understands horse herd etiquette) move away from all the members of the established herd. If his background has not been with horses who taught him horse herd etiquette, he might get it wrong and try to be assertive. There may also be poorly socialized horses already in the group who see any newcomer as fair game to chase and bully.

Therefore, it is important, when introducing a new horse into an established group, that space is adequate to allow the new horse to safely move away from all the other horses. It's also important that there are no areas where the new horse can be trapped and kicked or driven through a fence.

After a while, if the new horse shows suitable evasive behavior to indicate that he is not a threat, he may be accepted into the group. Horses are very definite about who they like and who they don't like. In some cases, the best that can be achieved is an uneasy truce.

Using a safe (not wire) fence between the horses, to establish contact and build relationships, often makes it easier and less traumatic. Another approach is to give the new horse time to feel at home by putting him into the main paddock by himself. Once he's had time to explore and distribute his scent, via droppings and urination, he will feel more established and comfortable in the area. Then the other horses can gradually be introduced into the paddock with the new horse, one at a time.

Sometimes it's easiest to divide a single large paddock with electric fencing. The new horse's area can be moved around until he is familiar with the whole space. At some point, you'll be able to see who might make a good buddy for the new horse and give them time together. With careful planning and ample time, the new horse can usually become part of the existing group.

Two people walking two horses in-hand on either side of fence can be a safe way to help establish the relationship.

If you have a helper, acceptance can also be more rapid if horses are taken for walks or rides together, or do ground work in the same area at the same time.

Horses can show profound jealousy. If you have a strong bond with a horse, he may show unhappiness about sharing you with another horse, so all introductions should be handled carefully, with sensitivity, and be given time to establish.

A horse new to the group may gradually work his way up in the group's social order if he has the intellect, age, good health and spirit to do so.

Two new horses greet each other by touching foreheads and noses. This may be followed by a sparring match (head-pushing, striking out) to see who can push who around. The point is to see who can get the other to move his feet backwards first.

Figure 22: These horses are meeting for the first time, or they are meeting again after a long separation. Each horse is checking out his possible status in relation to the other horse. You can see the focus, the overall body tension, the stiff ears and the tight lower lips. Photo Kelsey Corey

He who gives up ground first is lower in the social order at that point in time. This jostling for position is part of the enduring soap opera of horse group life.

It follows that any horse who assumes a higher level in the social order will be watchful and mindful about retaining his position. However, an accepted and trusted horse tends to collect a band of relaxed members.

Figure 23: The chestnut mare (Boots) asking the grey gelding (Smoky) to give way. She doesn't have to actually bite to get her message across. Her intent and body language are sufficient. In the seven years they were together, he always faithfully moved when she directed him to move.

The challenge for us is to infiltrate the horse's social system. To become part of a horse's in-group, we need to go undercover - become more horse-like. We can copy and mimic this whole equine process of accepting new group members.

It's not hard for us to become an undercover horse because quite a lot of horse herd etiquette shows up in the etiquette of human groups. The behavior of all mammal species living in groups has to balance the benefits of group living with the inevitable competition for resources. This is because all the group members need the same resources. When resources are plentiful, there is little need for competition. But when resources become scarce, rank in the social order becomes more important.

Most dominant behaviors we see in domestic horses are part of 'resource guarding'. If horses are fed hay or grain at specific times, these special deals detonate rank order confrontations which don't have a corresponding trigger in the wild. It could be compared to the frenzy people get into when big city shop doors open for the Boxing Day sales. People who usually behave normally suddenly unleash considerable violence.

The *Greet & Go* process that follows is based on how horses who know each other greet upon meeting. In this exercise, the horse can choose to greet us. If he decides not to greet us, nothing happens, so this exercise builds trust.

Greet & Go is an activity that we'll soon do every time we encounter a horse.

When I introduce this exercise to people, they invariably want to pat the horse's face after the horse has politely put his nose on their hand. In terms of horse etiquette, I have the feeling that horses find this distinctly impolite. Most horses dislike it, especially from a stranger. They often try to move their head away. Some horses have learned to stop people doing this by using their teeth if a warning with the ears is ignored.

As already mentioned, new horses greeting each other often put their foreheads together and push to help get the measure of the other horse (Figure 22). I think putting our hand onto the horse's face feels to them like a dominating gesture.

The *Greet & Go* exercise does not include any fondling of the horse's head or ears.

#76 HorseGym with Boots includes a demonstration of *Greet & Go* at work.

The Greet & Go Process

Figure 24: Smoky has put his nose on Bridget's hand. We always allow the horse to close the last two inches of space between his nose and our hand.

The *Greet & Go* exercise is simple but profound. You approach the horse from the front in a quiet, relaxed, friendly manner and before you quite reach him, you hold out your arm, palm downwards and invite the horse to touch the back of your hand. Your hand stands in as another horse's nose. Horses use their noses to explore like we use our hands.

As soon as the horse has touched your hand, which is the *Greet*, you quietly walk away. Walking away is the *Go* part of the process. You approach the horse, *Greet*, then immediately do the opposite, *Go*, by walking away. You are showing the horse that you respect his space and his place in the universe and in your life. You no longer approach his bubble only when you want to halter him and make him do things.

Figure 25: Boots is stretching out her neck to close the gap between her nose and Bridget's hand.

Figure 26: After Boots greets Bridget by putting her nose on Bridget's outstretched hand, Bridget immediately moves away. Note how she carries the swishies behind herself like a quiet tail and how she is deflating the energy out of her body.

Horses appreciate the opportunity to greet us politely. The act of turning and walking away (*Go*) is a neutral act a horse higher in the social order might do, i.e. say hello and then walk away and mind his own business because he is secure in his relationships. It shows that neither party is looking for any sort of further interaction or confrontation.

The whole dynamic is like the friendly recognition we give to colleagues as we walk past them at work or when we briefly greet a neighbor out shopping.

Here is an important point that runs through all our interactions with a horse. If the horse comes into our space (our bubble) of his free will, he needs to do so politely. If he's not polite, it's fair for us to send him away. If we go into our horse's space (bubble) we need to do so politely. If we intend to ask him to do something, we need to ask politely, giving the horse time to think about our signal and respond to it.

I suggest doing the *Greet & Go* routine as often as you can during your usual interactions with your horse. Approach the horse from the front offering your outstretched hand. A horse that wants to greet you will put his nose on your hand. As soon as he does, walk away and carry on doing what you were doing.

Figure 27: Bridget and Boots having a greeting during Quiet Sharing of Time and Space.

If the horse does not want to put his nose on your hand, that's okay too. Go away and carry on what you were doing. The horse will appreciate that you understood his feelings at that moment in time.

The greeting is also a good way to begin further contact, such as clicker training, grooming or getting ready for an activity.

If your horse does not want to greet you, you have instant feedback on his mood of the moment and can adjust your plans accordingly.

If the horse does not want to greet you (ignores you or walks off) you can choose to carry on the interaction by walking a loop away from the horse and approaching him again, creating another opportunity to offer your hand. Allowing the horse to say, "No," without consequences builds his self-confidence. It may take just a couple of approaches before he is willing to greet you, or it may take more than ten relaxed approaches spread over one or more sessions. Eventually he will. Meanwhile, you are learning how to relax yourself out of frustration.

Horses with unknown histories can have all sorts of reasons for not wanting to greet a person. If you make five or ten approaches every day and they are all rejected, keep a written log. At some point, it will happen. Celebrate quietly and *Go away*.

Remember, horses have all day every day. If you have the time and good humor to persist, the horse will eventually greet you. A treat offered after the greeting will amplify the importance of your offer to greet.

If you don't have all day, you might decide to simply go away. The horse misses out on attention and treats. Maybe you can openly give your treats to another horse before you go. Horses will observe this and think on it overnight.

If the horse usually moves away at your approach, you probably need to go back and spend more time with *Quiet Sharing of Time and Space* to build the bond. Work out if he is moving away due to anxiety or because he has slipped into a 'you can't catch me' habit. He may have benefited from this sort of avoidance behavior in the past.

If he seems to have reverted to a 'you can't catch me' habit, there are ways of making yourself more interesting. You could pay attention to other horses or pets or things. Sit down and eat an apple or a carrot. You could go back to *Quiet Sharing of Time and Space* and ignore him. If you've set up the environment for a one-on-one date, he will probably not like being ignored. Whenever something seems broken, go back to *Quiet Sharing of Time and Space* to re-forge the bond.

You can also, if your environment allows, hide behind trees, buildings, vehicles or barrels to pique your horse's curiosity. I had great fun running from tree to tree and hiding for a while behind each one. My horse couldn't stand watching this novelty without coming over to investigate. Make yourself interesting. Seek ideas outside the square.

The point of the *Greet & Go* exercise is that the horse is free to choose whether he wants to greet you. If you've approached him several times and he's wandered away rather than touch your outstretched hand, you are receiving a clear message.

The challenge becomes to consciously change your behavior and observe closely to see how the horse responds. How does his behavior change when you act differently? Such experimentation is fun. There is no right and wrong. At any time, your horse unbounded by ropes is free to choose what he thinks is the best thing to do at that moment.

These exercises allow you to see what works to your advantage and what doesn't. It's very different from making horses do things when you decide they'll do it because you have a rope on them or they are contained in a small area.

Used every time you approach your horse, the *Greet & Go* exercise helps build a powerful connection. If you include a gift with the greeting (food treat or a scratch and rub and eventually putting on the halter and going for a grazing walk), it becomes even more powerful. If you use clicker training, you can build the greeting habit using click&treat to begin with, and then click&treat occasionally.

When greeting the horse, or finishing a session with him, it is important that most of the time you turn and walk away, rather than the horse turning and walking away from you. It's a matter of protocol. You don't leave before the Queen or King. These seemingly small things are the nuts and bolts of maintaining social order between you and your horse.

Chapter 5 looks at how we can begin to influence the horse's actions with our body language.

Chapter 5

Becoming the CEO

The next two exercises, *Claiming the Spot* and *Watchfulness*, enable us to gradually improve and consolidate our social rank in our group of two. Harmony results when both the horse and the handler are clear about who usually decides what to do next when interactions begin.

Lounging in the paddock with our horse on a fine day is a wonderful pastime. However, most people also like to do other things with their horses. There will be times when horses must do unhorse-like things such as being attached to their handler with a rope, standing on three legs for foot care, being touched or rubbed all over, wear a rug or asked to travel in a small dark space.

To develop a domestic horse's confidence with things no wild horse would ever face, we have to form a relationship that places us in the position of the horse's CEO. The CEO is the one who has the plan. A good CEO not only has the overall plan, but he or she also listens carefully to other members of the group.

In our group of two, when we are with our horse, we have a plan about what we'd like to do. But the plan is flexible enough to cater for what the horse brings to the session. Some days we may decide the horse's ideas are actually the best plan for that day.

Our session plans have to work for us and the horse. If we don't want to have a constant two-way dialogue about what is happening, we should get a bicycle or a motorbike instead of a horse.

If we need something to happen for our safety or the welfare of the horse, a well-educated horse will do his best to comply with his handler's requests. But this can only happen if his handlers have put in the time and effort to give him the skills to do so.

Claiming the Spot and *Watchfulness* are developmental exercises. Once the horse understands them, they are not something we do often as specific tasks. The way our horse behaves during everyday activities tells us whether they are in good working order or in need of refreshing.

Exercise 4: Claiming the Spot

The *Claiming the Spot* exercise builds willingness to follow our suggestions. Most things people do with horses requires the horse to follow the person's suggestions.

You can begin the *Claim the Spot* exercise when you and your horse are comfortable with the first three exercises.

1. *Quiet Sharing of Time and Space* when you are sitting, reading or meditating.
2. *Active Sharing of Time and Space* when you are wandering about swishing your swishies outside of your horse's personal bubble.
3. Doing *Greet & Go*, i.e. approaching your horse from the front and he is usually happy to greet your outstretched hand.

With some horses, you may reach this stage in your first or second session. With other horses, it can take any time up to several weeks (presuming that you can spend time together most days). Relationships with horses, just like person-person relationships, can only grow and develop through time spent in each other's company.

Horses newly from the wild, or horses who have learned to fear people's actions, will present their own unique challenges.

With some horses, you may do *Claiming the Spot* only a few times because they are so naturally conscious of your position in their social order. Horses who tend to be bold and confident may need a few sessions to be convinced that moving off promptly and politely is the best way to handle the situation.

Claiming the Spot is an exercise we can return to whenever it might be helpful to remind the horse that usually we have the plan, and that it is in his best interest to follow our suggestions.

If you watch a group of horses interacting, especially if they are hungry and being fed hay or hard feed, it's easy to see which horse moves another horse off a particular spot.

The horse *Claiming the Spot* usually walks with quiet determination, head down, and (if the other horse hasn't moved yet) will pin the ears and snake the head and lunge to bite the other horse (if he's still there).

That's it. That's all you need to learn to do to *Claim the Spot* from your horse. You simply behave like another horse higher in the group social order. You use body language that the horse already understands.

Claiming the Spot Process

You can view *Claiming the Spot* in action in *#77 HorseGym with Boots*. There is also an older clip featuring Smoky called *Ex. 4: Claiming the Spot* in the *Universal Horse Language* playlist.

This series of three photos will help explain the process before we dive into the details.

Figure 28: Bridget is approaching Boots' side with strong intent to ask her to move off the pile of hay and go find another one. Swishies held behind like a tail.

Figure 29: As she gets closer, Bridget activates her swishies to give Boots a very clear signal that she wants to Claim that pile of hay. Bridget uses as much energy as needed to ensure that Boots moves away, but not more than she needs.

Figure 30: Boots accepts that Bridget wants to Claim the pile of hay and moves away to another pile. Bridget will get her chair and sit by the pile she has Claimed.

Safety

Claiming the Spot and <u>Watchfulness</u> can, for some people and horses, be the hardest of these exercises. Here are three key points to keep in mind.
1. Use body extensions long enough so you can strongly influence the horse (if necessary) from <u>well back</u> out of the kick zone. For the first few times, use a lunging whip or a stick&string combination.
2. Be sure you are mentally and emotionally prepared to ensure that when you ask the horse to move, you will follow through with determination until the horse does move. Most horses readily move on to another pile of hay when they realize that you are firm in your resolve to move them on. The first time you ask will be the hardest. You are the CEO. The plan is for the horse to move off that spot when you claim it.
3. Some horses will be much more resistant to giving up their spot than Boots and Smoky on the video clips. Unfortunately, we don't have their first responses on video. Once they understood our body language, they

easily moved when we asked. Most horses readily take the option of moving to another pile of hay.
4. Some horses will try harder to come back to the food you have claimed. Be prepared to watch closely and send them away with enough energy to convince them that you now own the spot you've claimed. Horses play these games with each other all the time. Some horses have personalities that like to test limits and other horses prefer to go with the flow for an easier life.
5. Make sure you have spent adequate time with the first three exercises, especially if the horse is new, and if you are new to horses.

Organizing the Sessions

It takes a bit of organizing to set up the *Claiming the Spot* exercise. Spread out several piles of hay spaced well apart in an area where, ideally, there is not much else to eat.

The best time to do this exercise is when the horse is usually fed hay. It helps if he is a little bit hungry. If you don't want hay on an arena surface, use big tubs, tarps, sheets or blankets (unless the horse is worried about these).

The very first time doing this exercise is the hardest part of the whole process. Once we know how it works, it gets easier.

It's impossible to quantify the amount of energy needed to move the horse off the hay the first time because each horse is different and each handler has a unique way of raising and lowering his or her body energy. It is a voyage of individual discovery.

1. Start with *Quiet Sharing of Time and Space* while your horse enjoys a pile of hay.
2. After sitting, reading or contemplating for a while, get up and walk <u>with precision and determination</u> toward the shoulder of your horse, holding your swishies behind you.
3. Be sure to move toward the horse's barrel or shoulder. You don't want to be directly behind or directly in front.

4. <u>Focus totally</u> on the horse. You must move with intent so strong that the horse moves.
5. A few meters away from the horse, <u>make your body as big as you can</u> by breathing in deeply, expanding your chest and rising up on your toes.
6. Keep walking and <u>direct</u> your horse away from the hay <u>with big sweeping motions of your arms and swishies</u>. Put your focus beyond your horse to where you want him to go.
7. As you bring your swishies into play, start softly and get as energetic as needed to get the horse moving off. HE MUST MOVE. <u>The instant he moves, drop your arms and your energy</u>. The drop in your energy tells the horse he's made a wise decision.
8. If he tries to come back to the same hay, go through the whole process again. Get big, direct him away with sweeping motions, adding intensity to the swishies until he goes off to find another pile of hay, at which point you relax by breathing out and deflating your body.
9. When you decide to move the horse off a particular spot, HE MUST GO. The idea is to use as much energy as required to move the horse off that pile of hay. He mustn't be allowed to come back to the same pile. It's now your pile of hay. Wave your swishies and jump up and down if that's what it takes to convince the horse to move away.
10. You have *Claimed the Spot* as your own. Stay relaxed. Get your chair and sit down at the Claimed pile of hay.
11. In between *Claiming the Spot,* sit and read or meditate, wander about with your swishies and, importantly, every now and then do the *Greet & Go* routine.

12. The skill is to find the balance between the *Greet & Go* and *Claiming the Spot* moves. If the horse greets readily but is slow to move off when you *Claim the Spot*, then do a bit more of *Claiming the Spot*. If the horse moves off a spot very readily but is a bit reluctant to greet you, then do considerably more of the *Greet & Go*. You can add a treat to the *Greeting* to give it more importance.
13. As long as you are consistent with how you approach the horse (side-on for moving him off and front-on for *Greet & Go*) he will soon take your orientation as a major part of your signal. The importance of body orientation is looked at in detail in my book, *Conversations with Horses*.

Figure 31: Bridget is approaching Boots from the front with her hand extended to offer a greeting. We alternate Claiming the Spot with the Greet & Go exercise.

The Shy, Timid, Flighty or Suspicious Horse

1. You could organize to have a timid-type horse already in your work area before you bring in the hay. If he is confident enough to approach you and the hay (or

follow behind you and the hay), you can drop some of the hay and walk away to make the next pile. This is huge for building a timid horse's confidence. Horses naturally tend to follow anything moving away from them, and move away from anything coming toward them.
2. If he is very anxious, experiment to find something for which he will approach you, e.g. a favorite food in a familiar bucket. Put it down for him and walk away (*Go* exercise).
3. It can work to have an armful of light-weight food containers with a bit of a treat in each one. Lay them out in a circuit as the horse follows you. He'll probably quickly work out the game of finding a treat in each container. Once you've laid out all the containers in the circuit and the horse has followed you polishing off the treats, walk around it again and adding a treat to each container as you go. You can do this as long as the horse stays interested.
4. As the horse's confidence develops, gradually stay longer at each dish before you walk on after dropping in the treat. You have success when he is able to stand right beside you at the dish waiting for you to toss in the treat.
5. When your timid horse will eat his special ration out of a bucket in your lap, you know you have made massive progress.
6. At some point, the horse will show enough confidence for you to use piles of hay instead of the containers.

General Points

Your aim is not to run the horse off his pile of hay. Your aim is to use just as much energy as you need to get him to move on. Using several piles of hay means that the horse always has somewhere positive to go, so there is little reason for him to be upset that you are *Claiming the Spot*. This exercise builds your horse's willingness to follow your suggestion to move away.

This exercise, done with precision and feeling, has a huge influence on how your horse thinks about you. The harder it is to initially have the horse move at your request, the more profound your influence. During the teaching and learning phase, it may take considerable energy to move a bold, confident, imaginative horse.

The first time I did *Claiming the Spot* with Smoky, he looked at me as if to say, "You and who else is going to move me off this lovely bit of hay?" I had to be able to say, "Me and my swishies are going to insist that you leave this hay to me and go find another pile."

When you first begin this exercise, there is no time for double guessing. The first time I did it with Smoky, I had to use considerable swishy activity to get him to move off. The second time, he realized it was much easier to just move to another pile of hay. He realized, a) that I wasn't going to chase him and b) there was always another pile of hay to go to.

As you repeat the process over several days, you will probably notice that the horse reads your intent at your approach. He'll begin to leave the hay as soon as you breathe in and make yourself large. This is much more a mental game than a physical game. The horse learns that he can make you relax and deflate by moving away.

We can only *Claim the Spot* if the horse is eating hay or grazing, drinking or resting in a favored shady spot. In other words, the horse needs to be standing still and doing his own thing. You then decide that you would like that spot for your own reasons, and ask him to move away.

If your horse approaches a trough with the intention of drinking, and you are in the vicinity with your swishies, take the opportunity to claim the water first, pretend to drink, then politely invite him to have his turn. Doing this just once or twice consolidates your position as higher in the group social order.

If the horse is timid, you could move away and let the horse claim the water first, to strengthen his self-confidence around you.

Timid horses also gain confidence in you if you protect them from other horses by sending the other horses away.

Exercise 5: Watchfulness

The second exercise, *Watchfulness*, will consolidate your position as CEO.

Horses in group situations are constantly aware of the position and movements of the other horses. A subordinate horse generally moves away at the smallest focused glance, ear flick or tail swish directed at him by a horse higher in the social order. It is very much like workers in an office keeping an eye on the mood, presence or absence of the boss, and adjusting their behavior accordingly.

This is why social order or hierarchy is such a powerful system to help keep the peace among a group of animals who all have the same needs from the environment. Their instinct to compete for the resources is tempered by their need for safety in numbers and the security of other group members with specific skills and knowledge.

As CEO, we need to ensure that the horse applies this same *Watchfulness* to us. We gain *Watchfulness* by acting like a horse (or boss) who is ensuring that his subordinates remember their positions. *Watchfulness* strengthens your horse's desire to focus on you.

It is essential to consider horse behavior in relation to its development on arid grassland environments over millions of years.

For prey animals, there is safety in numbers because it lowers the probability of becoming a meal for predators. For group-living predator species such as wolves and lions, group cooperation increases the probability of catching a meal.

Some horse-keeping people like to play down or deny the existence of social rank order or hierarchy among horses. While observations of feral horses suggest that horse social order may be relatively flexible rather than linear, denying that it exists is not helpful.

During times of plenty, social order is less noticeable than during hard times. We can observe the same differences in human society. When there is plenty for all we can envision utopias. As resources become scarce, altruism turns into survival behavior.

The Process of Gaining Watchfulness

While your horse is eating at one of several piles of hay (or if he is grazing) quietly walk around the horse outside his bubble. Walk far enough away so the horse remains unconcerned.

As you walk an arc behind the horse, check to see if the horse is watching you. With eyes set either side of the head, horses can see almost 360 degrees including when they are grazing. If their head is straight they have a blind spot directly behind their tail.

How often you do the *Watchfulness* process depends on the nature of the horse. For some horses once or twice is enough, if you do it well the first time. Other horses will need a few repeats over several days to be convinced that it is in their interest to keep a *Watchful* eye on you. Every horse is different.

#78 and *#79 HorseGym with Boots* illustrate *Watchfulness.* Clip *#78* demonstrates the 'First Action'. Clip *#79* demonstrates the 'Second and Third Actions'. There are also some older clips in my *Universal Horse Language* playlist.

Figure 32: I'm approaching Boots from behind. She doesn't swing around to face me, but she is looking back to keep an eye on what I am doing.

*The First Action

If we can see the horse's eye, then the horse can see us. For this 'First Action' we are looking to see if we can catch the horse out for not watching where we are. Some horses may never give us an opportunity to catch them out. They are naturally *Watchful* and you need to do very little for this exercise. Other horses may not see us as important enough to keep an eye on before we learn to use this exercise.

If the horse is being *Watchful* you can expect him to move his head or his body when he notices you slipping into his blind spot. Some horses will turn to face you when you get behind them.

If you've stood a few seconds in the blind spot right behind the horse and you can't see either eye (so he can't be seeing you) and he isn't moving so that he can see you, you have an opportunity to zip in for a stealth attack with your swishies and chase him off the spot with lots of energy. Be sure to use your swishies and stay well out of the kick zone.

We make this stealth attack into a game. Our part of the game is to get good at noting when we can't see the horse's eye on us. The horse's part of the game is to be *Watchful* all the time, so we can't catch him out. Once we've chased him off, we go back to resting in our chair and enjoying the universe while the horse goes back to grazing or nibbling hay.

Occasionally, get up to walk arcs behind the horse to check his *Watchfulness* again. Be careful to walk beyond the horse's personal space bubble. As soon as he makes a noticeable effort to keep you in view, back up a bit, turn and walk your arc in the other direction. If you can do these arcs two or three times without getting another opportunity to chase the horse off, the exercise is done.

Intersperse walking the arcs behind him with approaching from the front in a friendly manner (with treats handy) to do a *Greet & Go*.

Figure 33: Although she is grazing and I am behind her, I can see Boots' left eye. If I can see either of her eyes, she is watching me, whether her head is up or down.

Figure 34: I can't see either of Boots' eyes, so she is not watching me. I'm in her blind spot so this is the moment to zip in and briskly ask her to move off.

Figure 35: I can see Boots' right eye, so she is watching me even though she is grazing and has her tail to me. This is not a time I would ask her to move off.

If you are walking big arcs behind the horse and you can see that he is watching you all the time he is eating, even if he just moves his head, you can leave the horse to enjoy his food.

Figure 36: Bridget is walking an arc behind Boots to check her Watchfulness. You can see that Boots has her head turned to keep a close eye on what Bridget it doing.

Confident horses who tend to be pushy around people could get caught out 'not watching' several times before they gain true *Watchfulness* around you. Anxious type horses whose flight instincts are closer to the surface will not be caught out very often. When this basic *Watchfulness* using several piles of hay is strong, you can begin to work with the second action.

*The Second Action

#79 HorseGym with Boots illustrates the Second and Third Actions.

For this, you have only one pile of very desirable hay or a container of special feed in your enclosed area.

Repeat the process as for **The First Action** above. However, because there is not another food pile for him to move to, the horse may argue a little bit. If he is a bold, confident horse, he may run around with high energy, like Boots did when we first worked through this exercise.

Figure 37: I've claimed the bucket of food from Boots. After briefly checking to make sure I meant it, she cavorted away before stopping and looking at me politely.

Done well, this exercise has a profound influence on the horse and there is seldom a need to do the *Second Action* more than two or three times. These pictures are from the first repeat I did with Boots, to get some illustrations, several years after we first did them.

After you've moved the horse off the food, Claim it as your own. This is a version of *Claiming the Spot*. As soon as the horse asks politely, invite him back to the food.

Figure 38: After running a couple of circles after I claimed the food, Boots stopped and looked at me in a polite manner.

Figure 39: As soon as she stopped and looked at me politely, I invited her back to the food. Notice how her head has come down compared to the previous picture.

After doing this exercise, she yielded the food bowl to me every time I asked. For the 'Third Action', coming up, we ask to *Claim the Spot* with minimal energy and the horse promptly responds by moving away quietly.

At first, during the 'Second Action' just described, the horse may repeatedly try to come back to the food, especially sneaking in behind your back. Simply hold your position at the food, keep your eye on him and send him away again. Apply as much energy as you need to send him away, but not more than you need. We just want the horse to understand that the food belongs to you once you have Claimed it.

Eventually the horse will stand looking at you with ears forward, asking you a question about what he should do next (Figure 38). Politely invite him back to the food by either moving back and drawing him to the food, or going to greet him and walking him back to the food (Figure 39). Then ease yourself away and let him eat.

Over several sessions, experiment with walking big arcs behind the horse to see if he keeps his eye on you the whole time. If you are in his blind spot and he is making no attempt to keep an eye on you, chase him off again. Once you've Claimed the food, he needs to wait well back and look at you, at which point, invite him back to the dish or pile of hay.

As mentioned earlier, each horse's response will vary depending on his character type, his previous experiences and the nature of the relationship he has with the handler. Character type is looked at in more detail in my book, *How to Create Good Horse Training Plans*.

When he remains *Watchful* each time you allow him back to the food, it's time for your 'Third Action'.

*The Third Action

While the horse is eating, make yourself big and quietly, but with determination, walk toward his neck/shoulder. Firmly ask him to surrender his food to you, exactly as you did for *Claiming the Spot*.

Have your swishies between you and the horse. Use as much energy as you need to be effective to move him off the food and leave it to you.

Your aim is to be able to quietly as him to yield the food three or four times in a row. Each time the horse moved away politely pause briefly, then invite him back to the food.

This exercise is an extension of *Claiming the Spot* (Exercise 4) where you used multiple piles of hay. However, now you are Claiming the only desirable food source in your enclosure, so you are confirming your senior position in the horse's mind in a stronger way.

Key Points

When you've claimed the food, focus on it but watch the horse with your peripheral vision. He may run around you or try to come back and reclaim the food (in which case you send him away again), or he may stand and face you politely. Be aware that he could also stand and face you in a challenging manner, usually behind you, so you need to clearly read what the horse is saying. If he seems to be in a challenging frame of mind, briskly send him away again.

There is more information about 'reading horses' and horse body language in my book, *Conversations with Horses*.

As soon as you see the horse standing politely with ears forward, approach him from the front and greet him, then step beside his neck and politely indicate for him to move forward to the food. Alternately, you can walk backwards away from the food and draw the horse forward to it.

You know you have consolidated your senior position when each time you approach the horse in the same determined way, he politely and quietly moves and allows you to have the food. You keep possession of the food until he shows a polite waiting manner, at which point you invite him back as explained above.

When it takes very little energy on your part for the horse to quietly yield the food to you three times in a row, and he returns politely on your invitation, you have achieved this exercise to a good standard. Check this game out every now and then, or when you feel you need to ensure your position in the social order.

Having your horse automatically give way to you in this situation will make him much safer to be around. It is up to you to read your horse and check regularly to see if you still have a high level of *Watchfulness*.

If your horse is truly *Watchful*, his head will swing up to check your movements every time he sees you, no matter how far away you are. If you can see your horse, he can see you. Your horse will learn to recognize your car or your appearance in the distance and respond with interested *Watchfulness*.

Figure 40: Smoky is checking out to see who is coming and what they might want.

Once you know in your bones how this exercise works, the rules that helped you to learn it become flexible. You do what feels right in any one situation to maintain your safe, positive relationship.

Figure 41: Watchfulness: Boots is keeping a close eye on what Bridget is doing.

So far, we have learned the first five exercises.
1. *Quiet Sharing of Time and Space*
2. *Active Sharing of Time and Space*
3. *Greet & Go*
4. *Claiming the Spot*
5. *Watchfulness.*

We use these five exercises interchangeably to create a dynamic situation where the horse learns to easily read our body language. To enhance the horse's awareness of what we are doing, we balance *Sharing of Time and Space* (*Quiet* and *Active*) plus *Greet & Go* with *Claiming the Spot* plus *Watchfulness.*

Here is an example of how a session using the first five exercises might flow. In this example the horse would be grazing or eating hay at one of various piles.

1. Start with *Quiet Sharing of Time and Space.*

2. After a while of reading, drawing or meditating, wander over to approach the horse from the front and do a *Greet & Go.*

3. Return to your chair and read a bit more, watch the clouds or meditate.

4. Wander around the enclosure gently swishing your swishies and taking note of how large the horse's personal bubble is today. Make sure that if you run into his bubble you immediately move further away from him.

5. Return to your chair.

6. Approach the horse from the side and ask him to move away from the pile of hay or the grazing spot. Fetch your chair and sit at the spot you have claimed.

7. Wander over and approach the horse from the front and do a *Greet & Go.*

8. Return to relax in your chair for a while.

9. Walk arcs behind the horse to see if you can find a moment when you are in his blind spot and he is not keeping his eye on you, so you can zip in and chase

him off. If you can walk three or four arcs behind him and he remains watchful, return to your chair.
10. Wander over and approach the horse from the front and do a *Greet & Go*.
11. Wander around the horse's home gently swishing your swishies and taking note of how large the horse's personal bubble is right now. If you run into his bubble, immediately move further away.
12. Wander over and approach the horse from the front and do a *Greet & Go*.

With a few days' practice, you will find your own rhythm to work through the five exercises in a quiet, low-key way. You'll mix up the order of events in a way that suits you, the horse and the environment you are working in.

You'll get better at raising and lowering your energy level. You'll become more consistent in the different ways you approach the horse for *Greet & Go*, *Claiming the Spot*, or when you are checking for *Watchfulness*.

The more consistent you are, the easier it is for the horse to read your body language and know what your intention is. Once he clearly understands your intentions, you have given him the confidence that comes with knowing what to expect.

Chapter 6 looks at the last three Universal Horse Language exercises. They allow us to move with the horse.

Chapter 6

Moving Together

Exercise 6: Guiding from Behind

If you watch the interactions of horses in a group, it's easy to see horses higher in the social order moving subordinate horses by approaching them and using pressure to get them to move their feet. The horse doing the hazing follows behind for as long as he wants to keep the other horses moving.

Figure 42: The horse on the right is sending a clear message of, "Move on," to the two horses on the left. Photo by Carol Nudell

It's this willingness to respond to a request to 'move on' that we want to foster. Interestingly, when we ride, this is exactly what we are doing: *Guiding from Behind.*

If we can teach our horse to be comfortable with *Guiding from Behind* on the ground, he'll have a huge head start if we want to ride or drive in harness. He will already know voice and body energy signals for 'walk on' and 'halt'. He will be relaxed with the idea of his handler giving signals from behind his withers.

Once the horse knows it well, *Guiding from Behind* is an exercise we can apply to daily interactions.

Figure 43: Riding is nothing more than Guiding from Behind, sitting on the horse rather than walking along on the ground.

The Process of Guiding from Behind

Rather than break up the written information with photos, I've put in a selection of photos illustrating the process before we get to the details.

#80 HorseGym with Boots demonstrates the process. Some older clips can be found in my *Universal Horse Language* playlist.

Figure 44: Bridget has asked Boots to yield her pile of hay and she is walking behind Boots for a few steps as Boots moves on to another pile of hay.

Figure 45: Bridget is walking behind Boots to the next pile of hay. Note Bridget's swishies behind her body like a quiet tail when she is not using them to amplify her body language.

Figure 46: As the horse begins to understand the exercise, follow behind for longer. The easiest way to do this is to spread the piles of hay further apart each session.

Figure 47: Bridget is using her body language and voice "Whoa" signals just as Boots is going to halt at the hay anyway. Note Bridget dropping her hips to accentuate the "Whoa" body language. Horses easily see what we are doing behind them. The Watchfulness exercises ensure that Boots will have her left eye firmly on Bridget.

Figure 48: When Guiding from Behind is smooth between piles of hay, we can generalize into grassy paddocks. Bridget uses her body energy to keep Boots moving. Once the horse is tuned in to our body language, we seldom need to use the added energy of the swishies.

Figure 49: Bridget is using her "Whoa" voice and body language signals. Boots understands that she can stop and graze when Bridget asks for the "Whoa". The grass acts as a reward, so Boots will be very alert to the "Whoa" signal. Bridget will wander away for a while.

We can begin *Guiding from Behind* when the previous five exercises are smooth.

Exercise 1: During *Quiet Sharing of Time and Space*, the horse remains relaxed. He is comfortable eating hay or grazing close to you. He may come over and greet you. If your horse has a pushy personality, you can easily ask him to stand back with your swishies or move your chair to enlarge your personal space.

Exercise 2: During *Active Sharing of Time and Space*, the horse remains relaxed while you wander around the paddock. He is not worried when you activate your swishies beyond his personal space bubble. The horse accepts you sitting in your chair or wandering around as he would accept the actions of another horse in the paddock.

Exercise 3: Your horse accepts an offer to *Greet & Go* at least 90% of the times you extend your hand for a greeting. You have made it a habit to offer a greeting every time you meet up with a horse.

Exercise 4: When you ask to *Claim the Spot* from your horse, your body language is clear and consistent. The horse understands your intent and moves away willingly.

Exercise 5: You have worked through the three actions of the *Watchfulness* exercise. You have a good feeling for how sensitive your horse is. You know whether your horse is naturally watchful or if he might occasionally need a reminder about the importance of keeping an eye on you.

The *Guiding from Behind* Process in Detail

1. Start the session as usual, with *Quiet* and *Active Sharing Time and Space,* in an area where you have set out several piles of hay. It is easier to learn this using piles of hay rather than a grassy paddock because walking between piles of hay gives the horse specific destinations when you ask him to walk on.
2. Check that you have the horse's *Watchfulness* as you walk arcs behind him while he eats at a hay pile. You know the horse is *Watchful* if you can't find any moments in his blind spot when he is not watching

you. If you can see his eye, he can see you. *Guiding from Behind* evolves out of *Claiming the Spot* and *Watchfulness*.
3. *Claim the Spot* from your horse using the minimum energy needed. By now you can hopefully approach the horse's side with clear intent and he moves off by reading your body language.
4. If it still takes a lot of energy to move the horse, spend more time with the first five exercises. *Claim the Spot* and *Watchfulness* need to be smooth before you head into *Guiding from Behind*.
5. Begin *Guiding from Behind* by *Claiming the Spot*, then as the horse moves toward another pile of hay, walk along behind him for a few steps in a quiet, relaxed manner (see Figures 44, 46 and 48). Stay well out of the kick zone.
6. Keep the swishies held behind you, like a tail, unless you are using them to amplify your body energy.
7. If the horse turns toward you, use the swishies to redirect his front end until he is moving away from you again. A Parelli-trained horse may think that pressure behind means you want him to turn around and face you as in the Parelli 'catching game'. It's important to be sensitive to any other training in the horse's past. If you don't know his past, give him the benefit of the doubt.
8. If he halts, also stop and pause for a moment, then use your body language and swishies (if needed) to ask him to move off again toward a new pile of hay. If you do this exercise when the horse is usually fed hay, he will probably move easily to the next pile. Some horses might become anxious about you walking along behind them, in which case, proceed slowly.
9. When you begin, follow behind for only a few steps before returning to your chair. If the horse seems anxious, hang back a bit more at first. As his

confidence grows with repetitions, you can walk a bit closer to him, but always stay beyond the kick zone.

10. For this part of the exercise, keep your body energy low and your body language totally relaxed as you walk behind the horse at his pace.

11. Return to your chair for a while. After a bit of reading or contemplation, repeat the procedure: claim the hay he's eating and as he walks away, follow behind for a few steps before returning to your chair.

12. Intersperse the *Guiding from Behind* with frequent *Greet & Go* (approaching horse from the front and maybe offer a treat after the greeting), followed by walking away and resting in your chair for a while.

13. Each session, put the piles of hay further apart, which will automatically give you more steps walking behind the horse to the next pile.

14. When the horse feels comfortable with you walking behind for a few steps, gradually increase the number of steps before you leave him to his hay while you wander about the enclosure in a relaxed manner, or go back to your chair. Eventually you can walk behind the horse all the way to the new pile he has chosen.

15. Stay with this exercise for several sessions until you can ask the horse to move using very little energy and he willingly moves off in a relaxed manner and stays relaxed as you walk behind.

16. If the horse stops between piles (he may want to poo, wee or have a scratch), wait a few moments, then ask him to move on again. Always use a soft first signal. Begin with body language, then bring in the swishies as necessary. Use only as much energy as needed (but enough to be effective) to get him to quietly move off again.

17. As mentioned earlier, if he turns toward you, put energy toward his front end to show him that you want him to turn away and walk on. If you are gently

persistent in redirecting the front end, and <u>remove all pressure the instant the horse turns away</u>, you will rapidly build the new communication.

Building in the "Whoa" Signals

1. When the moving off and following behind pattern feels smooth, it's time to build in the "Whoa". As you walk behind the horse, just as he is about to stop at the next pile of hay, say, "Whoooaaaa," and drop your body energy. Glide back into a halt yourself, as you say it, by tucking your butt under yourself and dropping your hips as you stop (see Figures 47 and 49). I say "whoa", but you might use a different word or sound.
2. You can follow the "Whoa" with a *Greet & Go,* offering a treat after the greeting. You want to show him that "Whoa" is a great thing to do. Anyone can make a horse go, but can you have him halt at liberty when you ask?
3. When the horse shows you that he understands the "Whoa" voice signal really well, use your energy to ask him to walk right past the first pile of hay he comes to, and ask him to "Whoa" at the next one. Relax and go rest in your chair. It may take several sessions over several days until this part of the exercise is smooth for both of you. It's always better to have multiple very short, successful sessions rather than try to repeat the new task many times in one session.
4. When your communication feels strong, start asking him to trot between piles. Raise your body energy first, then, if you need to, bring in the swishies to get the trot. Relax the energy as soon as the horse trots. Keep up the use of your "Whoa" as well.

5. When it feels right, string several requests of, "Please move off," and "Whoa" together before you turn and walk away to rest in your chair.
6. Make it more challenging as you both get better. Perhaps you can eventually ask for a walk to the first pile, a trot to a second pile, then ease back into a walk to get to a third pile.

Directional Suggestions

1. When the horse willingly walks past one or two piles of hay and listens for your "Whoa" signal to stop, gradually add in directional signals.
2. Decide which pile of hay you want him to go to. Ask him to move and then use arm gestures, body language and the swishies to indicate the direction you'd like him to take. Remember to drop your sending and directing energy as soon as the horse moves in the direction you want. You can always bring your energy up again to repeat your signals. The only way the horse knows he's doing what you want is if you instantly drop your energy of intent as soon as he complies.
3. If you train with clicker training (see Appendix 1), you can add a click&treat when the horse reaches the pile you had picked out. With clicker training we can also teach voice signals for left and right turns.
4. You may find that the horse turns easily in one direction, but not so easily in the other direction. This is normal and due to natural asymmetry. Like us, horses are right-handed or left-handed. Working a bit more on the harder side helps even things out. The handler usually also finds it harder to give clear signals using the non-dominant side of his or her body.

5. Gradually incorporate more dramatic changes of direction.

Generalization

1. When the horse understands the concept of *Guiding from Behind*, you can guide from behind in other situations, without the piles of hay. If the horse turns toward you, put energy toward his neck or shoulder to show him you want him to move away from you. Do it slowly. Stay well back. There's no rush. Remove your energy as soon as he indicates he'll move away. You can always bring your energy up again if he hesitates.
2. If you use clicker training and your horse is mat savvy, it works well to use mats as destinations. As the horse prepares to halt his front feet on the mat, use your voice "Whoa" signal. Appendix 1 provides a summary of how to get started with clicker training horses. More information is available in my book: *How to Begin Equine Clicker Training*.
3. You can also work in a grassy paddock, allowing the horse to graze for a while after you give the "Whoa" signal, while you relax into *Sharing Time and Space* for a while (see Figure 49).
4. Be sure to breathe out and deflate your body as part of your "Whoa" signal. When you get a halt in response to your "Whoa", celebrate hugely by following it up with a *Greet & Go* with treats attached. If you do clicker training, a triple treat or jackpot would fit in here.
5. If the horse doesn't stop for your "Whoa" signals, amble behind him in a casual way until you can see that he is going to stop. Say "Whoa" and celebrate by walking forward in a relaxed manner and giving him a treat. If you don't have treats in your pocket, walk to a stash of treats you've set out earlier and get him one. He may follow you, which means he's seamlessly

moved into the next exercise, *Shadow Me*. If you then time your "Whoa" signals to the moment he begins to stop with you at the treat stash, he'll understand what you want very quickly.

6. To further establish the "Whoa" signals, I use *Guiding from Behind* in a training area where hay or grass is not a distraction. I immediately follow the halt with a click&treat, going to the horse to deliver the treat. I like the horse to halt on the 'click' and wait for me to come to him to deliver the treat, rather than have him turn around. If you do not use clicker training, you can follow the "Whoa" with a *Greet & Go* accompanied by a treat.

7. *Guiding from Behind* is useful when asking your horse to move around during daily management. Often, it's much easier to grab the swishies than to go through the whole halter and rope ritual. *Guiding from Behind* can build into sending your horse into a truck or trailer while you stay outside the door. It gives you the communication to ask the horse to move in front of you through water or a narrow space.

Exercise 7: Shadow Me

Horses seem instinctively drawn toward movements that invite them along. If one senior horse in a group moves off purposefully, intent on going to water or setting out for new grazing, the other horses usually follow.

In the *Shadow Me* exercise, the horse synchronises with us because he wants to. We can indicate a turn toward the horse with a hand signal and a turn away from the horse by obviously shifting our weight. The choice to stay with us (or not) belongs to the horse. *Shadow Me* is a learned behavior that we will cherish and use forever.

Horses moving together are totally aware of the speed and direction of the other horses near them. If you watch a group of horses galloping freely, they never run into each other. They turn and swerve as a united body, similar to the schooling of fish. It is this connectedness that we would like to emulate, very modestly, with the *Shadow Me* game.

How much the horse wants to stay with us depends on how attractive we can make ourselves. It depends on how well we convince him that we are heading somewhere of interest to him. Walking between stashes of treats gives most horses a clear reason to stick with us.

Figure 50: Bridget and Boots are heading for a container of treats. Boots is happy to walk with Bridget to the container. Note that Bridget is in the process of saying, "Whoa", and dropping into her hips as she halts. Boots is walking along with Bridget in the Shadow Me exercise.

The *Shadow Me* Process

This exercise develops naturally from the *Guiding from Behind* exercise, if all the other exercises are in good shape. Our prerequisite is that the horse halts at "Whoa" signals when we are *Guiding from Behind* in an area where food is not a distraction.

#81 HorseGym with Boots demonstrates the process.

As mentioned earlier, I reinforce the halt with a *Greet & Go* followed immediately by a treat. If you use clicker training, you would click on the halt and move up to the horse to deliver the treat.

1. **Start with *Guiding from Behind*, then ask for a "Whoa"**. Walk forward to the horse's neck and indicate with your body language that you would like him to come with you to walk to a stash of treats. He may well come with you.
2. If he doesn't follow you, walk to your treat stash, get one out of the container and go back to the horse and give it to him. Then again ask him to move along with you to walk to the same treat stash.
3. At first you may need to use your body language and your swishy (to put a bit of pressure into the air behind you or by gently tapping his hind end) to show your horse that you want him to move along with you. To tap his hind end, have your swishy in your outside hand and reach behind without changing the 'walking forward' orientation of your body.
4. Repeat *Guiding from Behind* followed by a halt, move to his shoulder and ask him to come with you to get a treat out of a container. If you do this several times, the horse usually gets the picture quickly. He may have already learned this exercise during *Quiet Sharing of Time and Space* if you kept treats in stashes away from your chair and he came with you to get a treat when he stood back nicely.
5. It's important to have stashes of treats in various places (at least three or four places) so that the horse doesn't expect to go to the same place all the time. If you mix up which stash you walk to, he'll work out that it's good to come along at your suggestion

because you know where the containers are, and you can open them.
6. We use the treats to strengthen our attraction and to help the horse understand what we want more easily. We are giving him a purpose and a 'wage' for being a willing partner.
7. If he chooses not to follow (lack of willingness), return to *Guiding from Behind* and any other earlier exercise that feels broken.
8. If trust seems to be missing, do more *Greet & Go*.
9. If there seems to be a lack of focus, do more *Watchfulness*.
10. If willingness to follow your suggestion could be improved, do more *Claiming the Spot*.
11. If your two-way bond or relationship feels frayed, do more *Quiet Sharing of Time and Space*.
12. When the horse chooses not to come with you, avoid demanding or pleading with him to come. Simply keep moving in the direction you were already headed and ignore the horse.
13. If you want to do a reset rather than end the session, gradually move yourself into position behind him in a way that does not give the horse the idea that he's wrong. Stay relaxed. The horse is allowed to make the decision to come with you or not. Once you are behind him, use the *Guiding from Behind* exercise, followed by a "Whoa" and another invitation to walk with you. In other words, begin again. If he's not willing the second time, wait until another day.
14. With experience, you will get better at reading the horse and choosing the best pace and route to keep the horse interested in walking with you. You'll also begin to know when he feels like playing and when he doesn't. If he loses interest, pause, turn away, rest. Maybe do something else. Even better, learn to stop

before he loses interest. Usually that will make him keener next time.
15. Every moment you spend with a horse is different. There is never a time when you stop reading the horse and adjusting your responses and requests.
16. If you use clicker training (see Appendix 1) you can easily build duration of walking together with the following exercise. It is demonstrated It is demonstrated in *#83 HorseGym with Boots* and in a clip called *Shadow Me Game at Liberty* in my *Universal Horse Language* playlist. Clicker-savvy horses often love to play *Shadow Me* as long as the treats hold out.

Walking Together: Building Duration
Ask the horse to walk beside you for one step: halt, click&treat.
Ask the horse to walk beside you for two steps: halt, click&treat.
Ask the horse to walk beside you for three steps: halt, click&treat.
Ask the horse to walk beside you for four steps: halt, click&treat.
Ask the horse to walk beside you for five steps: halt, click&treat.
Carry on building up this pattern as long as the horse remains interested.
You may be able to add two steps each time, then eventually maybe add five steps each time.
If the horse loses interest, exit gracefully and leave it until a new session.
If you get to twenty steps, you've achieved a great deal

and it's time for a major celebration.

Doing a little bit often (up to 20 steps) usually makes this a favorite game.

Figure 51: Bridget and Boots walking together in the Shadow Me exercise.

Generalization

As you and the horse get to understand and feel comfortable using the *Shadow Me* exercise, you can build in transitions such as:
- walk-halt-walk
- walk-halt-back up-walk
- walk-trot-walk
- trot-walk-halt-back up-walk
- trot-halt.

Start with short segments of these and increase their duration and complexity as you and the horse gain confidence in each other.

Sometimes it's easier for the horse, at first, if he is between you and a safe boundary fence because that cuts out the option of swinging his hind end away. However, be careful not to push him toward the fence with your body's energy without realising that you are doing it.

Working in a lane is also excellent. *#39 & #40 HorseGym with Boots* are video clips that show detail about working in lanes.

Training Plan 8 in my book, *How to Begin Equine Clicker Training* is all about using lanes.

If the horse's energy comes up too high for your comfort when you ask for trot, definitely set up a lane to work in. The horse moves in the lane and you stay on the outside of the lane. Even a lane of rails on the ground will be helpful.

Figure 52: Bridget and Smoky playing Shadow Me at the trot.

If you use clicker training and the horse is mat-savvy, use mats as destinations. The mat you are heading toward will act as an environmental signal for the horse to come to a halt. *#6-#11 HorseGym with Boots* (inclusive) look at using mats.

#84 HorseGym with Boots demonstrates using nose targets and mat targets along with clicker training to build a solid habit of moving along together.

As skill and confidence increase, set up obstacles and markers and ask the horse to stay beside you doing some of these patterns:

- 90-degree, 180-degree and 360-degree turns
- weaving or serpentines
- figure-eights
- four-leaved clover
- over things
- under things
- between things
- through things.

Stay with one pattern until the horse understands it well, before moving on to another pattern.

Shadow Me is a fun way to bring a horse in for tacking up, or just to spend time with him. If he comes to your whistle and then plays *Shadow Me* to the tack room or *Sharing Time and Space* area, you don't need your halter and rope. You reward the behavior you want with treats and relaxation.

The whole phenomenon of human connection with horses is a balancing act between you directing the horse and the horse freely and willingly shadowing your movements or moving at your suggestion.

Exercise 8: The Boomerang Frolic

The *Boomerang Frolic* allows us to send our horse away at walk, trot or canter and invite him back to us. What a horse does when we send him away with energy will be totally unique to each horse. High energy horses may head out with great vigour and love a gallop around. Energy-conserving horses often take longer to work up enough adrenalin to move briskly.

The *Frolic* can be a hard exercise to get our head around because it requires that we fully relax and let go of all our expectations. It requires that we are prepared to be totally in the moment with the horse. Once learned, it is an exercise we can do any time we have good footing and the horse is willing.

The *Frolic* is all about learning from experience. It is about observing, noticing, comparing, experimenting. It is about trial and error and trial and success. There are only two rules. Rule one is to keep safe and expand your personal bubble with your swishies as necessary. Rule two is to always apply your energy to the horse's bubble in a way that starts with gentle suggestion and moves up the energy scale until you get the movement that the horse is willing to offer on that day.

Exuberant horses who love to move their feet can be feather-light to send into a *Frolic*. Confident, energy-conserving horses often need a bit more persuasion. Not all of us (human or horse) consider going to the gym as a priority. But it's still good to build exercise into our day to aid blood circulation, clear our lungs and get the muscles moving. A frolic is one way to raise breathing and heart rates with a horse at liberty in a safe, enclosed area.

To encourage a *Frolic*, we have to be effective about asking for movement, but we also have to give the horse time to recognize our intent and respond to it. We never want to suddenly startle the horse and trigger the reactive part of his brain. We want the horse to stay in the thinking and responding part of his brain.

Previous life experiences and training might make a horse dubious about *Frolicking* with you at first. To play like this, horses must feel confident, well fed and they need the bond with you that you have established by spending the time to get all the previous Universal Horse Language exercises working smoothly.

Boomerang Frolic Process

When your horse is comfortable with,

1. *Quiet Sharing of Time & Space*
2. *Active Sharing of Time & Space*

3. *Greet & Go*
4. *Claiming the Spot*
5. *Watchfulness*
6. *Guiding from Behind* including your "Whoa" signals
7. *Shadow Me,*

you can begin to suggest a *Frolic* which is Exercise 8.

#82 HorseGym with Boots demonstrates the Frolic exercise.

You need an area big enough so the horse can get up some speed but not feel trapped. On the other hand, you don't want it so big that he can get so far away that you can't influence his speed or direction. It's essential that the *Frolic* area you choose has good footing, as the horse may be moving at speed.

If your horse is generally happy to stay near you, round pens of 50' or 60' (18m – 20m) diameter can be useful but the area is a bit small for a full-sized horse, especially if he is a high-energy type. We don't want the horse to feel trapped. He needs to feel that he can make choices.

If possible, try different sized enclosures. Once you have established the exercise in a well-fenced space, you may be able to experiment with different sized areas using electric fencing materials (*not electrified*). It may be possible to set up an area with two corners and curved at the other end. A bit longer than wide is a good idea.

Corners give the horse somewhere to go if he does not want to play with you. This is perfectly okay. He is communicating with you. Just because you feel like playing doesn't mean he must feel like playing. It helps to play with a *Frolic* when your horse appears willing and energetic.

To start a *Frolic*:
- stand quietly beside the horse's shoulder, facing forward, and ensure you are both relaxed
- turn to face his shoulder and step back <u>well out of the kick zone</u> because an enthusiastic horse who enjoys this game may kick out as he departs

- bring your swishies, lunging whip or stick&string in front of you, so they are between you and the horse
- use clear body language (supported by gesturing with your swishies as necessary) and a voice signal to indicate that you'd like him to leave. Depending on the horse, he may stand there bewildered, walk off, trot off or canter off.

He may take your actions as an invitation to have a mad around the enclosure or he may not want to go far from you at all. Make sure your swishy is always in the hand closest to his tail when you are asking him to keep moving. This is your 'go hand'. Keep your body language as strong and active as necessary while you want him to keep moving.

Be sure to take into consideration any previous training (lunging, round-penning, Parelli Circle Game™) the horse may have had. If he is worried about leaving you, slow down and reward just a small willingness to move away from you. Invite him back very soon and give him a treat.

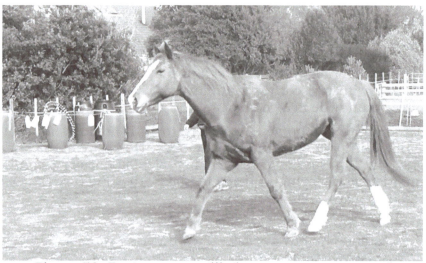

Figure 53: Boots now readily leaves me at a trot and sometimes offers a canter.

Gradually build up the length of time you ask the horse to stay out and moving. Gradually ask him to leave at a trot rather than a walk (if he doesn't already).

Each horse will have a unique way of expressing himself in such a situation. Be sure to keep yourself safe as the horse's energy comes up. Always carry your swishies or a stick and string or lunging whip in case you need to enlarge your personal bubble if he returns to you with abundant energy. Some horses enjoy being able to buck, kick up and cavort. You may seldom need to use your body extensions, but safety is always number one.

You'll learn to adjust your actions as you get tuned in to your horse and know what he is likely to do. The aim is to get the horse willing to move away at a snappy trot or canter. How long he stays away depends on the nature of the horse, but never let it be very long. It's better to send him out and call him back several times in a row, rather than ask him to stay out too long.

Figure 54: Boots is putting energy into active movement with nice self-carriage while out in a Frolic. She is an energy-conserving horse, so she's unlikely to gallop around with her tail in the air unless she has a good reason.

To ask the horse to return, step backwards away from him to draw him to you. Stop him at **arm's** length if he seems too enthusiastic as he returns. In this way, you build the *Boomerang* effect. You send him away and ask him to return to you.

Figure 55: The Boomerang part of the Frolic. I'm asking Boots to return to me by stepping backwards. I also whistle to let her know it's time to return. A whistle signal is useful when it's windy or the horse is far away.

If the horse gets excited and dashes off with an adrenalin rush, keep him out of your space and let him move until he returns to a state that allows him to become attentive to you again. Then you can draw him back. Emotional neutrality allows you to accept this behavior as the horse just being himself.

If he loses connection with you, keep your own flow of energy going and ignore the horse. Move and *Frolic* and dance about on your own. Music can help. It's fun to alternate between ignoring the horse and mirroring his movements at a distance.

At all times, be sure to stay out of the kick zone.

Eventually most horses clock back in emotionally and are willing to return to you when you ask. If not, dance away and end the session. A few minutes of play might be all he is ready for at this point. You can always start again later or another day.

To develop enthusiasm, give the horse a treat every time he comes back. If you use clicker training, you can also click&treat him for departures if he is not innately enthusiastic or wanting to leave you.

My horse, Boots, took quite a while to feel comfortable about being asked to move away from me with this free-style technique. She understood the process of lunging, but this was different. She is an energy-conserving horse with much more draw to stay near me than willingness to depart.

We use clicker training, so it made sense to click her for leaving me. I'd ask her to move a few steps away, click and walk to her to deliver the treat. It helped her realize that leaving me could result in good consequences just like returning to me resulted in good consequences.

If leaving us is easy for the horse, we can focus more on the returns. If leaving us is difficult for the horse, we put most of our early focus on having the horse leave with confidence. We build up his confidence to leave by asking him back very soon. Gradually, one second at a time, we ask him to stay out a bit longer by keeping our body language active for a bit longer.

Figure 56: Returning to me during a Frolic session always results in a good consequence in the form of a tasty treat. We can also use clicker training to show the horse that it is okay to leave us for a Frolic.

For a non-energetic type of horse, you can also increase enthusiasm by turning and running away from him to get his attention. Once he understands the dynamics of the exercise, you can use your body language and swishies to ask him to stay out longer and longer before you invite him back in.

At some point, he will probably realise that he has choices about where he moves and at what gait. Remember that for many horses, being given choices like this is unusual. It may take him a while to loosen up emotionally to become truly involved in a *Frolic*. It's also easy to do it for too long. Some horses begin keenly, but then get anxious. Read your horse carefully and if he changes from willing to anxious, stop the exercise and do something calming.

If you've come this far through the exercises, you will be able to work out how to develop your own special *Boomerang Frolic* with individual horses.

The idea of the *Frolic* can be generalised to include objects and obstacles to play with. We can also incorporate all kinds of movements and tricks we've learned to do at liberty.

Figure 57: We can generalize the idea of the Frolic to include objects and obstacles to play with.

If you have a group of horses and have taught all of them these exercises, it can be fun to send them out on a *Boomerang Frolic* together.

Once you use the Universal Horse Language exercises as part of your regular interaction with your horse, you will find that you can use the *Boomerang Frolic* to diagnose the strength of your relationship at the moment.

Keeping the Universal Horse Language exercises in good shape sets a strong foundation for the other things you want to do with your horse. The five 'forever' exercises are fun to use for warming up or cooling down.

The five 'forever' exercises are:

- Ex. 1 *Quiet Sharing of Time and Space*
- Ex. 3 *Greet & Go*
- Ex. 6 *Guiding from Behind* (this turns into Leading Position 6 as outlined in my book, *Walking with Horses: The Eight Leading Positions*.)
- Ex. 7 *Shadow Me*
- Ex. 8 *Boomerang Frolic* (when conditions allow).

Chapter 7 summarises what can be achieved with these eight Universal Horse Language exercises.

Chapter 7

Summary of the Eight Universal Horse Language Exercises

Learning and using horse body language has a huge overriding benefit in that the horse realizes that it is possible to understand people. The domestic horse is in the predicament of being held captive by a foreign species that speaks a foreign language.

When we use Universal Horse Language to 'speak' with our horse, he probably feels relief and delight similar to that of an English-speaking person in a remote country meeting up with another English-speaking person.

No doubt, we have a very strong accent when we use Universal Horse Language, but horses seem to recognize and appreciate our attempts. A horse who's had scary experiences with people may take longer to realize that we are trying to use a version of his natural language. Horses with limited or positive experiences with people are usually quicker to recognize our version of Universal Horse Language.

Let's have another look at what each of the eight exercises achieves.

1. Quiet Sharing of Time and Space

Figure 58: When we begin this exercise, we can sit in with the horse, or we can sit on the other side of the horse's fence, like Alex and Ada are doing here.

The only way to build and strengthen a relationship is to spend time together. We want to resemble the comfortable presence of another horse that belongs to our horse's in-group.

The purpose of *Quiet Sharing of Time and Space* is to be in the horse's presence over enough time to make us one of his crowd by forming a bond of familiarity. Spending ten, twenty or thirty minutes just sitting and relaxing with our horse, as often as possible, is something that we should never give up. It will hopefully become something that we do often. Many people find that sitting with their horse leads to a restful state of meditation.

Dogs who live in the house with their owners have the benefit of lots of time to learn to read their owners' habits and quirks. Horses tend to be treated more like bicycles or cars rather than members of the family. Sitting with our horse helps to address the fact that horses seldom see us unless we are feeding them or we want them to do something on our terms.

2. Active Sharing of Time and Space

Figure 59: Bridget is walking around Boots' enclosure gently moving her swishies back and forth. She is careful to stay outside of Boots' personal space. If the horse shows any concern, we immediately move further away.

With this exercise, we are emulating another horse moving around the paddock minding his own business. We don't want our active presence around the horse to be a constant ON signal. We want the horse to be comfortable doing his own thing as we casually stroll around his paddock doing our thing. We might also be there to fix a fence, pick up droppings or pull weeds.

For *Active Sharing or Time and Space* we stay active for a while, then have a rest in our chair. Every now and then we approach the horse for a *Greet & Go*.

Active Sharing of Time and Space is a 'developmental exercise'. This means that once the horse remains relaxed when we move around his enclosure, it has fulfilled its purpose. Unlike *Quiet Sharing of Time and Space*, we don't need to keep doing it on a regular basis. The horse will transfer the confidence he has gained into his everyday interactions with us.

3. Greet & Go

Figure 60: Bridget and Smoky greeting each other.

The *Greet & Go* exercise seems deceptively simple, but it has a profound effect on the horse if we use it consistently whenever we meet up with him. We may be approaching the horse to put on his halter and do stuff. Or the horse may be approaching us to see if he can initiate an interaction. Clicker-savvy horses are often keen to find out what game we have planned.

In either situation, the first contact should always be a greeting. While we are learning the *Greet & Go* exercise, we always *Go* away after the *Greeting*. We want the greeting to carry no expectation that the horse should do anything other than put his nose on our hand. Once the horse recognizes that we will always greet him in a friendly manner, he'll easily adapt it to the other things we do with him.

When I leave my horse parked somewhere, at liberty or tied up, I always greet when I return. Usually I click&treat after the greeting to reward the quiet standing. If the horse is waiting at a gate to be let out, I always greet before opening the gate.

Greet & Go is not a developmental exercise like *Active Sharing of Time and Space*. Greet & Go becomes something we do every time we move toward our horse or our horse walks over to see us.

Greet & Go does not include fondling the horse's face.

4. Claiming the Spot

Figure 61: I've claimed one pile of hay from Boots and she is walking over to another pile. My next move is to bring my chair to the pile I claimed and sit there for a while. To avoid grass seed on the sand, I used old electric blankets under the hay.

Once the horse readily yields his pile of hay, his grazing spot or his bowl of food, we only need to do this exercise occasionally if it seems to need refreshing.

I've generalized this exercise with Boots at feeding time. As I approach with her bucket to put it into place, she moves backwards several steps until I click and gesture that she can approach the bucket. Her feed is her treat in this situation.

We've generalized it even further around gate safety. When I open a gate, I claim the 'gate space' spot. She moves back several steps to earn a click&treat. Then I gesture for her to go on through the gate. This procedure is especially helpful if the gate swings inwards toward the horse.

Once the horse displays consistent politeness around food and yields the food to us willingly on request, we can modify our behavior. We can sit alongside the horse in a companionable way while he eats grass or hay. Horses who live together, and are not short on feed, often eat together

(Figure 62). We also want the horse comfortable eating from a bucket on our lap.

Figure 62: Horses who live together and are not short of feed often eat together. Resource guarding is usually a result of food shortage or keeping horses in highly unnatural, restrictive conditions. Photo by Kelsey Corey

Like *Active Sharing of Time and Space, Claiming the Spot* is another developmental exercise. We use it to create an understanding between ourselves and the horse. If we need the horse to move, we have developed clear body language signals that the horse accepts as information that he has to move.

Once the understanding exists, it remains the horse's habit as long as we consistently use the same body language. In other words, this is not an exercise we have to do all the time. The horse's willingness to move at our suggestion will color everything we do with each other on a day-to-day basis.

5. Watchfulness

Figure 64: As soon as we can see the horse, the horse can see us. If the horse looks forward to the time we spend with him, he will be on the lookout for us.

We first gain *Watchfulness* by asking the horse to leave a pile of hay or a bucket of special feed. We showed the horse that he needed to keep an eye on us, just as horses in a group keep an eye on each other.

However, with reward reinforcement, especially if we use a marker signal as in clicker training, the horse's *Watchfulness* includes a positive expectation that when he sees us, we're coming to do things that enable him to earn clicks and treats. Every session becomes a party to look forward to.

Clicker trained horses tend to be keen for their sessions to start and most are happy to keep playing until the treats run out. We can have short and frequent sessions on one topic or longer sessions with various activities interspersed with relaxation. Once the horse knows a variety of exercises, we can organize sessions so they include a selection of activities that help develop the horse emotionally, physically and intellectually.

The *Watchfulness* exercise, like *Active Sharing of Time and Space* and *Claiming the Spot*, are developmental exercises. Once the horse sees the value of keeping his eye on us, the habit will usually endure. We might occasionally set up a test to see if it is still as strong as we would like.

6. Guiding from Behind

Figure 65: When the horse is comfortable with direction from behind, we can generalize it to things like asking him to load up into a trailer simulation while we stay at the entrance.

We start teaching *Guiding from Behind* by walking behind the horse as he moves between piles of hay. Gradually we put the piles further apart. When the horse is relaxed about our moving presence behind him, we teach "Whoa" voice and body language signals by using them just as the horse is about to halt at the next pile of hay.

It gives us a way of teaching the essential 'walk on' and 'halt' signals with the horse at liberty and in a way that he naturally understands. The way we ask him to move resembles the way horses haze each other. We add our halt signals to his natural act of stopping.

We can generalize *Guiding from Behind* by encouraging the horse to walk between nose targets hung on fences or foot target mats laid out as demonstrated in *#84 HorseGym with Boots*. We can use it to ask a horse to move through a gate. And we can use it to keep the "Whoa" voice signal strong and refreshed. So, as well as being a developmental exercise, *Guiding from Behind* becomes one more helpful exercise in our kitbag of training tasks.

Relaxed *Guiding from Behind* builds a foundation for riding or driving. The horse will already be comfortable about direction from behind and know the key voice signals for 'walk on' and 'halt'. If the horse understands and accepts our ability to direct his movements from behind while he is at liberty, he will find further training much easier.

7. Shadow Me

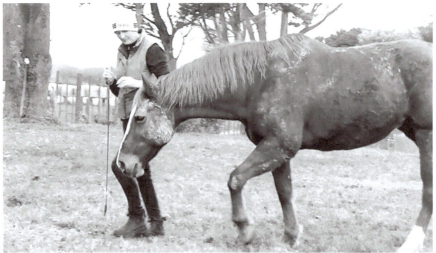

Figure 66: Boots is focusing strongly on moving with Bridget toward another stash of carrot strips.

Having the horse walk with us from point A to point B is a large part of our every-day interactions. To have the horse walk with us willingly at liberty means we have established a fair amount of trust and confidence.

When we do this by walking between stashes of treats, we give the horse a reason to come along with us that he can understand. It usually doesn't take the horse long to work out that we know where the various treat stashes are and that if he comes with us, there will be a positive consequence when we reach the next one.

By having treat stashes in three or more places, we can move between them over a variety of routes so that the horse has to read our body language and stay with us to get his next treat. In this way, we can establish the lovely habit of walking along with us before we put on a halter and lead rope.

We can generalize the *Shadow Me* exercise to walking together to pre-set nose targets hung on fences or pre-set foot target mats or special grazing spots away as demonstrated in *#84 HorseGym with Boots*.

#3 and *#4 HorseGym with Boots* further demonstrate these activities with halter and lead.

The *Shadow Me* exercise is much more than just a developmental exercise for Universal Horse Language. It sets the foundation for almost everything we want to do with our horse, from a companionable walk in the countryside, to daily care, to trailer loading and unloading, to riding or driving.

8. Boomerang Frolic

Figure 67: Smoky and Bridget having a Frolic.

Playing with our horse at liberty and at speed is fun. If we teach the *Frolic* with sensitivity and make sure we stay within the horse's emotional capability, the basic *Frolic* can be generalized to include free-form play with any of the movements we have taught the horse or that he offers.

By breaking the close connection of the *Shadow Me* exercise, and then re-forming it when we call the horse back, we strengthen the overall relationship. By letting go, we actually create a tighter bond. Letting go can be difficult at first. Doing it in tiny slices or increments allows us to achieve the enjoyment Smoky shows with his big trot in Figure 67, as well as the relaxation that Bridget shows as she admires her horse's movements.

Before you send the horse away, be sure you are standing well beyond the kick zone. A horse who plays this game with enthusiasm my kick up his heels in play mode. A horse playing with us expects us to be as quick and substantial as another horse.

The *Boomerang Frolic* is an exercise that will always be a work in progress. It will vary with time of year, temperature, venue and the mood of the horse. As you learn new things together, some of them can be incorporated into a *Frolic*.

Conclusion

That brings us to the end of the eight Universal Horse Language exercises.

1. *Quiet Sharing of Time and Space* (forever)
2. *Active Sharing of Time and Space* (developmental)
3. *Greet & Go* (forever)
4. *Claiming the Spot* (developmental)
5. *Watchfulness* (developmental)
6. *Guiding from Behind* (forever)
7. *Shadow Me* (forever)
8. *Boomerang Frolic* (forever when conditions allow)

Our job is to learn to emulate the body language of horses as best as we can. The horse will be relieved because we become easier to understand. We learn to keep ourselves safe, when the need arises, by enlarging our personal space by disturbing the air between us and the horse.

The horse learns that he is able to choose in his actions within our enclosure. He is not inhibited by the pressure of ropes and halters, which are totally foreign to natural horse life.

The horse is still inhibited by fences and we have to make sure that the fences are safe. We also have to read when a horse becomes anxious and be careful not to push harder so he contemplates running through or leaping over our fences.

We can use the Universal Horse Language exercises with a horse that has never been handled and we can use them alongside anything else we are already doing with our horse. The exercises are ideal to begin a relationship with any horse or to improve and consolidate an existing relationship.

I hope you have as much fun with them as Boots and I continue to have.

Appendix 1: Starting Clicker Training

Materials: Gear Checklist

1. A **training venue** where the horse feels comfortable. Ideally, his herd buddies are in view but not able to interfere.
2. The horse behind a **safe barrier**. This could be a non-wire fence or a gate or stall guard.

Figure 1: When starting a horse off with clicker training, it's wise to use protected contact, which just means keeping a barrier between you and the horse until you have established good table manners. Sometimes your only safe option might be to tie the horse up as in Figure 2. Protected contact allows you to step out of reach if the horse becomes over-enthusiastic.

Figure 2: Sometimes our only safe option is to have the horse tied up. Tying up with a wide halter is safer than tying with a rope halter in case something causes the horse to pull back. We're also using a Blocker Tie Ring. If the horse pulls back, there will be friction on the rope, but the rope can pull free completely, so the horse's whole weight won't be impacting the sensitive neck vertebrae.

You can find out more about the Blocker tie ring at: http://blockerranch.com/.

If the horse is tied up, make sure that he is able to relax when he is tied and that you allow him enough rope so he can easily engage with the target.

Protected contact allows you to stay safe if the horse becomes overly keen or excited about the idea of earning a tasty treat. You won't know how he will react until you try it out.

3. Decide on your **marker sound**; organize your mechanical clicker if you intend to use one. Having it on a cord around your neck or wrist means you can let go of it when you need to use your hand. But it also means you have to get it ready before you want to use it again so the timing of your click is accurate. I use a mechanical clicker sometimes to teach something new, but most of the time I use a tongue click. If you can't make a clear tongue click sound, a special short, sharp

word or sound (not used any other time) works just as well. For simplicity in these notes, I'll use the word 'click' to refer to whatever marker sound you decide to use.

4. You need a **pouch or pocket** that easily lets your hand to slip in and out. One of my favorites is a hoodie-style sweatshirt with a continuous front pocket that allows me easy access to the treats with either hand. Mostly I use a bum bag (fanny pack) type pouch.

5. The **treats**: people use tiny portions of carrot, apple, celery, grain, horse nuts, cereal, crackers, dry bread, popped popcorn — anything your horse likes. Individual pieces are often easier to manage than loose grain. Casual experimentation lets you find out which treats your horse likes best. My horse loves peppermints, so we use these for very special occasions like a superb response when we are learning something new. Often I have a variety of treats. Apple pieces score higher with my horse than carrot pieces.

Figure 3: It doesn't take long to get into the habit of getting the treats ready before heading out our horse.

6. You can **count out a specific number of treats** for a short training session or just have an abundant treat supply at hand. Running out of treats during a session is not a nice feel for the horse. I usually have spare horse pellets handy in a sealed container in case I need more.
7. You need a **hand-held target** to teach the horse that he has to *physically do something* (e.g. touch his nose to the target) in order to earn the click&treat. It's easiest to start with a target on a stick. A plastic drink bottle taped to a stick makes a nice safe, lightweight target. If the horse is nervous of sticks due to past experiences, a plastic bottle by itself, as in Figure 4 may be a better way to start. Some people use a fly swatter.
8. Ensure that the horse is **not hungry**. We want the horse to be interested, but not over-excited by the idea of special food coming his way.
9. If your horse is on restricted calories, ensure that his treats are counted as part of his daily total.

Two Extra Points

1. If the horse is wary about a new object like a target on a stick or a plastic bottle, I like to walk away backwards with the object (or have a helper walk away backwards with it while the horse and I follow together), and encourage the horse to follow until he makes up his own mind that it is okay to put his nose near or on the new item. Horses tend to follow things moving away and retreat from things moving toward them.
2. If you click by mistake, it's best to deliver the treat anyway. At this point you are training to give meaning to the click, so this is important. We want *the click and the treat* to belong together in the horse's mind.

Method

1. Simulation: Giving Meaning to the Click

It's ideal to learn the process of giving meaning to the click with a person standing in for the horse. The more adept we are with the mechanics of treat delivery before heading out to the horse, the more our horse will buy into our confidence that we know what we are doing.

1. Have your hand ready on the clicker (if using a clicker).
2. Present the target a little bit away from the person, so he or she has to reach toward it to touch it.

Figure 4: Learning the mechanics of the process with another person standing in for the horse means that the horse doesn't have to put up with our first fumbling as we work it all out. We have to get our head and our muscle memory around how to carry out the routine smoothly. If we approach the horse confident with what we are doing, the horse will buy into our confidence.

3. *Wait* for the person to touch the target with their hand (be patient).
4. The instant they touch it, click or say your chosen word or sound.
5. Lower the target down and behind your body to take it out of play.
6. Reach into your pocket/pouch for the treat (maybe use coins or bits of cardboard or mini chocolates).
7. Extend your arm fully to deliver the treat.
8. Stretch your treat hand out flat so it is like a dinner plate with the treat on it.
9. Hold your arm and hand firm so your pretend horse can't push it down.
10. When the 'horse' has taken the treat, pause briefly, then begin again with #1.
11. *Ignore* any unwanted behavior as much as possible.
12. Turn a shoulder or move your body/pouch out of reach if the person pretending to be your horse tries to mug you for a treat. Your 'pretend horse' has to learn that he or she earns the click&treat only by touching the target. If your 'pretend horse' is strongly invasive, put a barrier between you.
13. Multiple short sessions (up to 3 minutes long) at different times allow your brain and your muscle memory to absorb the technique, especially the finer points of timing.
14. If your helper is willing, let him or her be the teacher and you take a turn being the horse. Playing with being the horse is often a real eye-opener.

2. With the Horse

A: Giving Meaning to the Click: Touching a Target

The final goal is for the horse to move willingly to follow the target so he can put his nose on it to earn a click&treat.

First Session

1. Count about 20 treats into your pocket/pouch. Have a few spares handy in case you want to finish the session by putting a handful of treats into the horse's food bucket as an *end of session* signal.

2. Hold the target near his nose, but don't *thrust* it at him.

3. *Wait* until he touches even a whisker to it - *click* and *move the target* out of sight behind you. Moving the target out of sight will encourage his attention to the target when you present it again for the next repeat.

4. As you move the target behind you, simultaneously *reach for the treat* and deliver it away from your body by holding your hand out straight and rotating your shoulder to create a solid platform with your totally flat hand.

Figure 5: Deliver the treat with a flat hand and an outstretched arm so your body is well away from the horse. After the click, I move the target out of sight behind me to 'take it out of play'. It will then be obvious to the horse when I present it again.

5. If using a mechanical clicker, put your hand on the clicker ready to click.

6. Then hold out the target again. In your early sessions, put the target in the same place so you keep it easy for the horse to touch. At some point you will see that he really *gets* the connection between touching the target, the click, and the treat.

7. Repeat until you've used up your 20 treats. Ignore unwanted behavior. Stop after a good response. A few treats in a feed dish or on the grass is a nice way to let the horse know that one of your mini-sessions is finished. Put the target away out of sight.

8. Lots of short sessions (about 20 treats or 3 minutes) work well. You can do other things with the horse between the mini clicker training sessions.

9. Keep all your 'targeting criteria' the same until you get 10/10 confident repeats in a row, every time, over at least three consecutive sessions.

    By targeting criteria, I mean:
    - where you train
    - where you stand in relation to the horse
    - how and where you present the target.

Create a consistent end of session game that lets the horse know that the clicker training session is about to finish. Boots likes to finish with a series of belly crunches or touching various body parts to my hand. When I actually stop, I use a voice signal, "All gone," along with a gesture made by swinging my arms back and forth across each other at waist level several times. A handful of treats in a food bowl or on the grass is one way to signal that we're finished for now. To find out more about belly crunches, check out www.Intrinzen.horse.

Part B coming up shortly outlines how to make the target more interesting once the horse is totally ho-hum and consistent with touching his nose to the target when you hold it out near his nose.

The clip called *Clicker 1 with Smoky* in my *'Starting Clicker Training'* playlist illustrates the process of teaching the horse the connection between touching the target, the click, and the treat.

The method shown on the clip can be improved by not waiting so long to click&treat again. At first, it's good to click&treat often while the horse remains facing forward. In some parts of the clip we waited for Smoky to turn toward us and then turn away again before we clicked. That runs the risk of having the horse think that turning toward us first is part of what we want him to do.

B. Lunging for the Treat

Some horses are always polite, others not so.
1. Be safe. Put a barrier between you and the horse so you can move back out of range.
2. Make sure that the horse is **not hungry**. We want the horse interested in clicker work, but not over-excited or aroused by the thought of food treats.
3. Check out your **food delivery** method.
    a) Does it take too long to get your hand into and out of your pocket or pouch? Can you find easier pockets or a more open pouch?
    b) Do you move your hand toward your treats *before* you've clicked? This can cause major problems because the horse will be watching your hand rather than focusing on what you are teaching.
4. Be sure to only feed treats if they have been earned *and* you have clicked. Ask the horse to do something before giving a treat, either have him touch the target or take a step or two backwards.
5. Avoid feeding any treats by hand unless you have asked for a behavior and clicked for it. When not clicker training, put treats in a feed dish or on the grass.

6. Hold your treat hand where you want the horse to be rather than where he has stuck his nose. In the beginning, we want him to have his head straight to retrieve the treat. If he is over-eager, it can help to hold the treat toward his chest so he has to shift backwards to receive it.
7. If he lunges at your treat hand, take hold of the side of his halter after the click, so you have some control of where he puts his mouth. I also use a loud sharp, "Uh" (as in 'up') sound as a warning that the shark-like behavior is not what I'm after.
8. It can help to run your closed treat hand down the horse's nose from above, and ask him to target your fist before you open your hand so he can retrieve the treat.
9. It may also work to bring your fist (closed around the treat) up under his chin and have him target your fist before you flatten your hand so he can retrieve the treat. Often one of these little intervening steps can help build the habit of polite treat-taking.
10. A bit of experimentation will show you what works best with a particular horse.
11. With consistency and patience on the handler's part, over-enthusiastic treat-taking usually improves once the horse understands that a click&treat only follows when he carries out a request you have made. He'll learn that a treat will only follow if there has been a click first. That is why we have to be consistent.
12. The horse's character type will influence how he takes the treat.
13. Prompt, cleanly executed treat delivery is always important. Sloppy treat delivery is the first thing to look at if things are not going smoothly.

The clip called *Table Manners for Clicker Training* in my *Starting Clicker Training* playlist illustrates how we can use the timing of the click to improve the politeness around treat-

retrieval. The clip shows Smoky early in his clicker training education and Zoe who had never done it before.

C: Targeting: next sessions

#2 HorseGym with Boots shows the process in action. I would improve the technique shown in the clip by withdrawing the target down behind me, rather than over my shoulder, and standing rather than sitting. Also, not all horses are comfortable working across electric fencing, even if it is not electrified.

1. Once the horse is confidently touching the target held near his nose and seldom loses focus, gradually change the position of the target to make it more challenging for him. Chose one of: higher, lower, to the right, to the left. Teach him each of these one at a time. Each change you make is a big deal for the horse.

2. When he moves his neck to follow the target willingly and with interest, ask him to move a step to the right or the left to reach it. Stay with one direction until he is superb at it, then teach the other direction.

3. When he happily moves one step, gradually build up more steps. You can still be on the other side of a barrier while you teach this.

5. Whenever you change a criterion, begin by clicking for even the smallest hint of behavior heading in the new direction, until the horse shows confidence with the change. Then start withholding the click to gradually get more of what you want.

6. If he gets confused, *always be ready to backtrack* to the place where he can be continuously successful. This is the key to overall success and rapid progress. If he gives up because it's too hard, you have lost his willingness.

7. Stop each session on a high. Horses think about these things overnight. Stopping on a good note helps his motivation to do it again next time. Our tendency is to see if the horse can do it again right away, so we have to remind ourselves to stop right after the best response.
8. When you feel safe, work without the barrier.
9. Get creative to see where he'll happily follow the target (toward, over, between, into and around things).

D. Destination Training

Once the horse understands nose targets, we can hang them around our training area and use them to teach the wonderful habits of a willing 'walk on' and a prompt 'halt'. It operates equally well with ground-work or riding.

Each target becomes a destination that the horse understands. Walking between destinations becomes interesting for the horse because there is always a positive consequence (click&treat) upon reaching the next target.

A clicker-savvy horse soon appreciates the fact that we know the way to the next destination that will earn him a pause and a click&treat. It gives him a reason to want to go where we want to go.

If a horse is barn- or buddy-sweet, we can put out targets to gradually build confidence with moving a bit further away. At some point, the horse's thoughts will be more on seeking out the next target than on his buddies, barn or paddock left behind.

It may seem like a lot of effort at first, but once we have gained the horse's confidence about willingly going out and about with us, we can gradually reduce and then phase out the target props. We can use environmental markers (trees, corners, nice grazing spots) instead.

#3 - #5 HorseGym with Boots (inclusive) demonstrate ways of using nose targets in different contexts.

As well as nose targets, we can teach the horse about foot targets using small boards or mats or something like a Frisbee. We can use these as parking spots.

#6 - #18 HorseGym with Boots (inclusive) deal mainly with foot targets.

Figure 7: Boots is parked on a mat while Bridget models various positions in relation to the horse. The various positions are the subject of my book, 'Walking with Horses'.

We can set out mats as destinations or we can use something like a Frisbee to toss ahead of us, move forward to target it, toss it again, and so on. It's another way we can teach him confidence about leaving his home area. We create an activity that gives him something positive to do.

Providing destinations for my horses was a real breakthrough in how fast they learned and how willingly they applied themselves to learning new tasks that required moving from point A to point B.

Conclusion

For people who have never explored equine clicker training, using a nose target is a great way to start because when you no longer want to do it, you simply put the target away.

Once you get in the habit of having treats with you, and your horse becomes clicker savvy, you may be tempted to use the mark and reward clicker training system to teach your horse other new things or to refine tasks that the horse already knows.

Working for a food reward (even such tiny ones) activates one of the most powerful seeking systems in the deepest part of the brain.

Of course, horses learn readily by seeking out what will *release* signal pressure, i.e. the discomfort-comfort dynamic. But the motivating factor of a food *reward* allows us to add a whole new dimension to our training. The horse can become proactive in his communication with us. It's also a lot more fun to work with.

Once they are clicker savvy, horses show a strong desire to work for a food reward. They love the click&treat dynamic because the click (or special word/sound) can be timed to tell them exactly what they did that will earn the treat. Horses love clarity. They like to be right in the same way as we like to be right.

The mark and reward (clicker training) system removes much of the guess-work the horse is faced with when we use only the release reinforcement system.

Most horse-human dysfunction is due to lack of clarity coming from the human side of the relationship for these reasons.

1. Our behavior around the horse is inconsistent.
2. Our signals to ask the horse to do something are inconsistent and/or poorly taught.
3. We are not able to read the horse's body language well enough to understand what he is saying to us.

Most horses are happy to comply with our requests if we teach what we want carefully and ensure our signals are clear and consistent.

Clicker training has the handler looking for the moments to reward, rather than moments that need correction. As the handler gets better and better at thin-slicing a large task into its smallest teachable parts, it becomes easier and easier for the horse to learn by being continually successful.

We learn to reset a task rather than correct something that did not go as we hoped. This makes a huge difference to how horses perceive their training. Clicker-savvy horses often don't want their sessions to end. The positive vibrations that go with good clicker training make it fun rather than a chore.

As mentioned earlier, equine clicker training gives us a way to let the horse know instantly, by the sound of the marker signal (click), when he is right. It takes away much of the guessing horses have to do as they strive to read our intent.

A great deal more detail is available in my book, *How to Begin Equine Clicker Training: Improve Horse-Human Communication*. It is available via Amazon.com as an e-book or a hard copy book.

Appendix 2: List of YouTube Video Clips

Most of the video clips are shorter than five minutes, so they are quick to watch and easy to review if you are interested in specific tasks.

To reach my channel, put *Hertha MuddyHorse* into the YouTube search engine. The Clips are in one of three playlists.

1. Most of the clips are in my *HorseGym with Boots* playlist. Each title is written as *#? HorseGym with Boots*. For example, if you want to quickly find Clip number 22, simply put: *#22 HorseGym with Boots* into the YouTube search engine and it should come right up.
2. Some clips are in the *Free-Shaping Examples* playlist. These are named only, so to find a particular clip, go to that playlist and scroll down for the clip's name.
3. Other clips are in the *Thin-Slicing Examples* playlist. These are also only named, so you search the playlist for the title you want.

A list of all the current *HorseGym with Boots* Clips follows, as well as titles in the *Free-Shaping* and *Thin-Slicing* examples.

HorseGym with Boots Series

Topics are added to this series as they are created.
1. Introduction
2. Giving meaning to the click
3. Stationary nose targets

4. Parking at a nose target (also spooky new things to touch)
5. Putting behavior 'on cue'
6. Foot targets (also, free-shaping new behavior)
7. Backing up from the mat
8. Duration on the mat
9. Putting the mat target 'on cue'
10. Generalizing mats
11. Mat-a-thons
12. Chaining tasks
13. Anthem is new to nose targets (Anthem is a young quarter-horse)
14. Anthem is new to foot targets
15. Parking at a distance
16. The 'triple treat'
17. 'Walk-on' and 'halt' multi-cues
18. Parking out of sight
19. Free-shaping
20. The 'art of standing still'
21. Walk away for confidence (with new things)
22. Rope relaxation
23. Hosing on the mat (recognizing 'click points')
24. Parking commotions
25. Parking with ball commotion
26. *8 Leading Positions* overview
27. Good Backing = Good Leading
28. Leading Position Three (beside neck or shoulder)
29. Leading Position Three with a 'circle of markers'
30. Leading Position Three duration exercise
31. Natural and Educated body language signals
32. Sensitivity to Body language
33. Opportunity, Signals 1
34. Signals 2: Gestures
35. Signals 3: Touch
36. Signals 4: Verbal signals (also environmental signals, horse initiated signals and marker signals)
37. Signals 5: Intent
38. Signals 6: Body Orientation (of handler)
39. Train with a Lane 1
40. Train with a Lane 2

41. Leading Position Seven Clip 1 of 4, in front facing horse
42. Leading Position Seven Clip 2 of 4
43. Leading Position Seven Clip 3 of 4
44. Leading Position Seven Clip 4 of 4
45. Leading Position One: Clip 1 of 2 in front, facing away
46. Leading Position One Clip 2 of 2
47. Leading Position Two (horse's nose stays behind handler's shoulder)
48. Leading Position Eight Clip 1 of 7, Go, Whoa & Back (facing the horse's side)
49. Leading Position Eight Clip 2 of 7, Groom, Saddle, Relax
50. Leading Position Eight Clip 3 of 7, Drive-by Grooming & Mounting Prep
51. Leading Position Eight Clip 4 of 7, Side Step in Motion
52. Leading Position Eight Clip 5 of 7, Yielding Front End & Hind End
53. Leading Position Eight Clip 6 of 7, Side Step from Halt
54. Leading Position Eight Clip 7 of 7, Arc Exercise
55. Leading Positions Four and Five (beside ribs & beside butt)
56. Leading Position Four, Clip 2
57. Leading Position Six Clip 1 of 8, Liberty (behind horse)
58. Leading Position Six Clip 2 of 8, One long rein
59. Leading Position Six Clip 3 of 8, Square of lanes
60. Leading Position Six Clip 4 of 8, Rope Calmness
61. Leading Position Six Clip 5 of 8, Two Long Reins: Circle & Weaving
62. Leading Position Six Clip 6 of 8, 4 Leaf Clover Exercise
63. Leading Position Six Clip 7 of 8, 'Gates', Guided Rein, Obstacles
64. Leading Position Six Clip 8 of 8, Trailer Prep
65. Haltering process (with guided free-shaping)
66. Importance of Clear Signals
67. Prep 1 for Weaving, 90 and 180 degree turns; 'Draw' and 'Drive'

68. Weave Prep 2, 360 degree turns
69. Weave Prep 3, Weave a series of objects
70. Weave Prep 4, Only the horse weaves
71. Weave Prep 5, Curves, Circles, at Liberty
72. Ground-tie Clip 1, Getting Started
73. Ground-tie Clip 2, Another Venue
74. Thin-slicing a Trailer Simulation
75. Quiet Sharing of Time and Place
76. Active Sharing of Time and Place + Greet & Go
77. Claim the Spot
78. Watchfulness First Action
79. Watchfulness Second & Third Actions
80. Guiding from Behind
81. Shadow Me
82. Boomerang Frolic
83. Shadow Me Duration with Clicker Training
84. Shadow Me Using Targets

Thin-Slicing Examples

This playlist includes thin-slicing examples about the following topics. To find a specific clip, go to the *Thin-Slicing Examples* playlist in my channel and scroll down to find the one you want. New clips are added as they are made.

- Tunnel with Boots
- Pool Noodle task
- Head Rocking for Poll Relaxation
- Bottle Bank obstacle
- Zigzag for Horse Agility
- Yield Shoulder into a Turn on the Haunches
- Stepping over rails
- Soft yield to Rein Signals (5 Clips which also have their own Playlist)
- Thin-slice *'The Box'* Movement (back, sideways, forward, sideways)
- Backing up
- Rope Texting
- Thin-slicing the 1m board

- Water & Tarp obstacle
- Thin-slice the 'Shadow Me' Game at Liberty
- Free-shape Learning to Ring a Bell

Free-Shaping Examples

This playlist includes clips using the free-shaping technique to teach a task. To find a particular clip, go to the *Free-Shaping Examples* playlist in my channel and scroll down to find the clip you want. Most of these clips show both free-shaping and thin-slicing.
- Table Manners for Clicker Training
- Boots and Bicycle
- Bob meets Bicycle (Bob is a young quarter horse)
- Introduction to a saddle (with Bob, his first meeting with a saddle)
- Head-lowering (2 Clips)
- Clicker 1 with Smoky
- Smoky and Dumb-bell target
- Boots picks up the Dumb-bell
- Free-shape Learning to Ring a Bell

There are also short playlists on specific topics including:
- Thin-slicing the Wagon-wheel obstacle
- Teaching the S-bend
- Soft Yield to Rein Signals (5 clips)
- Hula Hoop Challenges (5 clips)
- Single Obstacle Challenges
- 2012 Horse Agility
- 2014 Horse Agility
- 2015 Horse Agility
- 2016 Horse Agility

Most of the Horse Agility clips have a commentary explaining the tasks and showing where we lost marks. Each task is marked out of ten, five points for the handler and five points for the horse. Some are at liberty and others are with halter and lead.

Reference List

Abrantes, Roger. DVDs (2013). *The 20 Principles all Animal Trainers Must Know.* Tawzer Dog LLC. www.TawzerDog.com

Budiansky, Stephen. (1997). *The Nature of the Horse: Their Evolution, Intelligence and Behavior.* Phoenix; London.

Burns, Stephanie. (2002). *Move Closer Stay Longer.* Parelli Natural Horsemanship; Pagosa Springs, Colorado. (Excellent if you feel nervous around horses.)

Camp, Joe (2011). *Training with Treats: with relationship & basic training locked in, treats can become an excellent way to enhance good communication.* 14 Hands Press; USA.

DeJohnette, Farah. www.fdhorsemanship.com.

Dorrance, Bill and Desmond, Leslie. (2001). *True Horsemanship Through Feel.* First Lyons Press; Guilford, CT.

Hanson, Mark. (2011). *Revealing Your Hidden Horse: a revolutionary approach to understanding your horse.* (Amazon On-Demand Publishing; www.amazon.com.)

Intrinzen. www.Intrinzen.horse (Accessed 30 Sept 2016.)

Kurland, Alexandra. www.theclickercenter.com

MacLeay, Jennifer. (2003). *Smart Horse: understanding the science of natural horsemanship.* Blood Horse Publications; Lexington, KY.

Miller, Dr Robert M. (1999). *Understanding the Ancient Secrets of the Horse's Mind.* The Russell Meerdink Co. Ltd.; Neenah, WI. (Also, look up Dr Miller to find his resources on Foal Imprinting if you'd like to know more about that.)

Parelli, Pat and Linda Parelli. www.parelli.com

Pryor, Karen. (1999). *Don't Shoot the Dog: the new art of teaching and training.* Bantam; New York. (About much more than dogs.)

Pryor, Karen. (2009). *Reaching the Animal Mind: Clicker Training and what it teaches us about all animals.* Scribner; New York.

Pryor, Karen. (2014). *On My Mind: reflections on animal behavior and learning.* Sunshine Books Inc; Waltham, MA.

Resnick, Carolyn. (2005). *Naked Liberty: Memoirs of my Childhood: the language of movement, communication, and leadership through the way of horses.* Amigo Publications; Los Olivos, CA.

Royal, Cynthia. https://www.facebook.com/cynthiaroyal.discoverthemagic.

Schneider, Susan M. (2012). *The Science of Consequences: how they affect genes, change the brain and impact our world.* Prometheus Books; New York.

Vandenborre, Karine. (2011). www.horsefulnesstraining.com